PRAISE FOR *ALIENS IN AMERICA*

"Here's the only guide there is in your search for America's UFO hot-spots. This is a fascinating book filled with all the facts and travel information you'll need, whether you're a UFO hunter or a skeptic; written by America's foremost UFO authority, William J. Birnes."

—JOEL MARTIN,
AUTHOR OF *HAUNTING OF AMERICA*

"Having lectured about flying saucers in all fifty states, I can testify that there is great interest in sightings and the sites where they occurred. *Aliens in America* provides very useful information about both. Bill Birnes proves there are many more interesting UFO sighting sites than just Roswell. People often know more about the sightings than their locations. Roswell is not next to Area 51; this book provides the scoop about both."

—STANTON FRIEDMAN, NUCLEAR PHYSICIST,
COAUTHOR OF *SCIENCE WAS WRONG*

"Here's your one-stop handy travel guide to UFO hotspots around the country from an investigator who has traveled these roads on his own. Bill Birnes is a longtime chronicler of UFO tales. He knows the stories and the players, but also where to stay and how to get there."

—GEORGE KNAPP, KLAV-TV NEWS,
COAST TO COAST AM RADIO TALK SHOW HOST

D0111279

ALIENS IN AMERICA

ALIENS IN AMERICA

A UFO Hunter's Guide to Extraterrestrial Hotspots Across the U.S.

WILLIAM J. BIRNES

Publisher of *UFO Magazine*,
and Host of *UFO HUNTERS*

Avon, Massachusetts

Copyright © 2010 by William J. Birnes
All rights reserved.
This book, or parts thereof, may not be reproduced in any
form without permission from the publisher; exceptions are
made for brief excerpts used in published reviews.

Published by
Adams Media, a division of F+W Media, Inc.
57 Littlefield Street, Avon, MA 02322. U.S.A.
www.adamsmedia.com

ISBN 10: 1-4405-0628-0
ISBN 13: 978-1-4405-0628-4
eISBN 10: 1-4405-0872-0
eISBN 13: 978-1-4405-0872-1

Printed in the United States of America.

10   9   8   7   6   5   4   3   2   1

Library of Congress Cataloging-in-Publication Data
Birnes, William J.
Aliens in America : a UFO hunter's guide to
extraterrestrial hotspots across the US / William J. Birnes.
p. cm.
Includes bibliographical references and index.
ISBN 978-1-4405-0628-4 (alk. paper)
1. Unidentified flying objects—Sightings and encounters—
United States—Guidebooks. 2. Extraterrestrial beings—United States—Guidebooks.
3. Human-alien encounters—United States—Guidebooks.
4. United States—Guidebooks. I. Title.
TL789.B558 2010
001.9420973—dc22
2010022578

This publication is designed to provide accurate and authoritative information with regard to the subject matter covered. It is sold with the understanding that the publisher is not engaged in rendering legal, accounting, or other professional advice. If legal advice or other expert assistance is required, the services of a competent professional person should be sought.
—From a *Declaration of Principles* jointly adopted by a Committee of the American Bar Association and a Committee of Publishers and Associations

Many of the designations used by manufacturers and sellers to distinguish their product are claimed as trademarks. Where those designations appear in this book and Adams Media was aware of a trademark claim, the designations have been printed with initial capital letters.

This book is available at quantity discounts for bulk purchases.
For information, please call 1-800-289-0963.

Dedicated to my wife,

NANCY HAYFIELD,

the editor-in-chief of *UFO Magazine* and Filament Books

and cohost of *Future Theater Radio*,

who does more jobs in an hour

than most of us do in a week.

ACKNOWLEDGMENTS

To Nancy Hayfield, the editor of *UFO Magazine* from whose research this book is largely assembled. Dedicated also to the writers and columnists for *UFO Magazine*, to our guests at *Future Theater Radio*, and to all of the UFO investigators in organizations such as MUFON, CUFOS, and NUFORC who keep the field alive with new information. Dedicated especially to the work of Dr. Bruce Maccabee, whose photo research and analysis has helped refute the constant onslaught of debunkers.

CONTENTS

CHAPTER SEVENTEEN. 1950s CONTACTEES AND THE INTEGRATRON 186
Landers, California

CHAPTER EIGHTEEN. THE MAURY ISLAND INCIDENT. 194
Maury Island and Vashon Island, Washington

CHAPTER NINETEEN. THE TRENT PHOTOGRAPHS 203
McMinnville, Oregon

FOREWORD

HOW UFO SIGHTINGS BECOME NATIONAL NEWS: THE TRENT PHOTO CASE

BY DR. BRUCE MACCABEE

Numerous UFO sightings occurred in the late 1940s and early 1950s throughout the great northwest of the United States. Perhaps the most famous sighting of that time period occurred in the farmland some miles south of McMinnville, Oregon.

It was just about sunset on May 11, 1950, when Evelyn Trent saw a strange object traveling roughly southwestward through the slightly hazy evening sky. She, at first, thought it was a parachute drifting sideways and falling, but then she realized there was no one hanging beneath it. As it got closer she called for her husband Paul to get the camera. As the object slowed he took two of the most famous UFO photos ever from his backyard before the object zipped away to the west.

Afterward, they didn't think too much about the sighting and waited a week or so to finish the roll of film before having it developed. A week or so later, a friend took the pictures to the local banker who put them in his bank window. The photo editor of the local paper saw them, thought they were interesting, and went to the Trent house where he found the negatives under the sofa! He studied the negatives, and—taking into consideration the good character of the

Trents—published them in early June 1950. Immediately they were a national sensation and, being the best UFO photos to that date, have since appeared in hundreds of UFO books and magazine articles.

Unlike most UFO photos that show distant, small, indistinct objects in the sky, the image of the UFO in the Trent photos is relatively large and sharply outlined. It is clearly not a manmade flying machine of that era, not a balloon or blimp, not an airplane or glider, not a helicopter . . . and not a parachute. What makes the Trent photos important for study is that they are so clear that they must be either a hoax or the "real thing," an "alien flying object" (AFI).

Over the years, skeptics have tried to explain the Trent case as a hoax. They know the Trents did not use the fancy photo manipulation that is sometimes used to make modern UFO photo and video hoaxes. Since there is no evidence of image blur caused by rapid rotation—as one would expect if it were a thrown model or a "Frisbee"—the skeptics claim that the Trents used a string to hang a small UFO model under the power wires that appear at the top of the picture. That would mean it was a bit more than a dozen feet away from the camera.

An astronomer, William Hartmann, who worked for the 1967–1968 University of Colorado UFO study (published by the Air Force in 1968 as *The Scientific Investigation of Unidentified Flying Objects*), studied the photos. He found no indication of a supporting thread. He used photographic and atmospheric theory and measurements of the original negatives to estimate the distance of the camera to the object. He calculated that the UFO could have been thousands of feet away and therefore large—perhaps thirty feet in diameter—and obviously not a model. He concluded that the Trents were probably telling the truth.

The skeptics responded to Hartmann's conclusion by pointing out that he hadn't taken into account veiling glare—a particular photographic phenomenon that would make the calculated distance shrink to zero. I reanalyzed the original negatives and found that both Hartmann and the skeptics had forgotten a surface brightness correction factor which, when included in the calculation, once again confirmed that the Trents had photographed a distant object. Thus the photographic and optical physics of the sighting supports the Trents' claims.

I scrutinized the whole McMinnville case, combining the most complete photo analysis ever done with the life history and character of the Trents. Besides talking directly to Evelyn many times in the 1970s, I interviewed others who had known the Trents for years. Everyone referred to the Trents as honest people who would never hoax anything. I concluded that the Trents told the truth and therefore the object was an AFI. (For the complete analysis, see *www.brumac.8k. com/trent1.html* and *www.brumac.8k.com/trent2.html*.)

The Trents died in the mid-1990s. During their last interview in the early 1990s they affirmed once again the truth of the story they had told more than forty years earlier and subsequently many times.

For more about the Trents, the McMinnville Sightings, and travel tips just for the UFO enthusiast, read Chapter 19!

INTRODUCTION

From Roswell, New Mexico, to Portsmouth, New Hampshire, the United States is dotted with UFO hotspots dating back to the 1940s. In 1947, Kenneth Arnold saw a flight of UFOs cruising in formation over Mount Rainer in Washington State just days after Harold Dahl saw a formation of flying saucers hovering low over Puget Sound. Folks in Washington DC, saw UFOs buzzing through the skies and read the headlines in local papers that the United States airspace had been invaded by flying saucers just five years later. And the entire world saw Movietone Newsreels of flying saucers swirling around the United States Capitol Building.

If you lived in New York during the 1980s, you might have seen huge flying triangles making their way up and down the Hudson River Valley. A decade later, the residents of Nevada and Arizona were treated to a dazzling show of floating boomerangs over the entire valley from Henderson, Nevada to the Mexican border. Gamblers on the Las Vegas strip, when they're not looking at rolling dice or spinning roulette wheels, occasionally look up to see strange lights zipping over the city from nearby Rachel, Nevada, near the home of Area 51. And the fishermen sailing off the Florida panhandle and into the Gulf also see strange configurations of lights in and over the water.

You don't have to be UFO investigator to enjoy a relaxing weekend combing for UFO remnants on Puget Sound. Nor do you need any special clearance to watch the UFOs dance in the nighttime sky above the "Alien Highway" outside of Area 51. Are they extraterrestrial? Are they our own secret weapons? Either way, travelers who've spent nights on that desolate stretch of country road have come back with amazing stories of huge triangular craft that hover motionless over the road and then zip away like the *USS Enterprise* going into warp.

There's even more to the stories of U.S. UFO hotspots. Many of the incidents that turned sleepy towns into beloved landmarks come complete with their own after-stories, denials, and debunkings. Residents have suffered through the planting of false evidence and staged personal character attacks. The hardship and heartache tell people involved in UFO research that there has to be something there. As an old prosecutor friend of mine once asked, why deny a crime if you never committed it in the first place? Applied to UFO research: why bother to debunk a UFO sighting if there are no UFOs to debunk? You'll see what we mean in some of the UFO stories in this book.

There are so many UFO hotspots in America that enthusiasts and vacationers looking for out-of-the-ordinary excursions often need a user's guide to the most historic UFO landmarks and the best places to take awe-inspiring UFO videos. And now it's here. Whether you are driving, camping, flying, or taking scenic train trips, this is your guide to find UFO hotspots, make hotel or motel reservations, find campsites for trailers and RVs, learn which airports are closest so you can book your airline reservations, and rent campers or cars.

UFOs might have traveled thousands of light-years to reach earth, but you can reach their landing spots in a matter of hours or days just by using this handy guide.

CHAPTER ONE
BETTY AND BARNEY HILL'S INTERRUPTED JOURNEY

A QUIET PAIR

Barney and Betty Hill were a very private couple. Spouses in a mixed-race marriage, uncommon enough in New Hampshire in 1961, they both worked for social causes in addition to their regular jobs. Barney worked for the United States Post Office and sat on the local Civil Rights Commission. Betty was a social worker, and both of them were members of the NAACP. At the dawn of the 1960s, a time before the civil rights movement began in earnest under President Johnson, the last thing the Hills wanted was national publicity. But that was exactly what they got—the cover of *Look Magazine*—when they had the misfortune to spot a huge bright light in the sky following their car along a lonely country road outside of Groveton, New Hampshire, on September 19, 1961.

FOLLOWED IN THE DARK

The Hills had been vacationing in Quebec and were driving home to Portsmouth in the darkness when they first spotted the light. Betty believed that it was one of the satellites, maybe Telstar, that the United States had just launched. Barney, however, thought that it was a plane that seemed unusually bright against the very dark sky. But the light seemed brighter than a conventional aircraft and it seemed to be tracking them, making Barney—who suffered from hypertension—nervous.

Betty insisted it was a satellite and urged Barney to stop the car so the couple could get out. Betty pulled out a pair of binoculars and got a better look at the object against the light of the moon. It wasn't a satellite at all, she realized, but something else: something that was illuminated with multicolored lights.

Betty said years later that she and Barney had the feeling that the object had suddenly noticed them. They became nervous, all alone on that New England country road at night.

BETTY AND BARNEY HILL

The Hills got back in the car and headed home. But the object matched their speed, and what had been eerie before was becoming downright frightening.

A CONFRONTATION

The object seemed to track them for a few more miles and then began a sudden descent toward their car. It stopped and hovered about a hundred feet above the vehicle, directly in front of the windshield. Barney stopped in the middle of the road, grabbed the pistol he had been carrying, and took the binoculars for a better look. He later said that the object hovered and then seemed to lower right above the road. Barney approached the craft.

Through his binoculars, he could see actual humanoid figures looking at him through the windows. Barney didn't know what this thing was, where it was from, or why it was parked about fifty feet in front of his car on a dark New England country road, but he could see figures inside. They looked too much like humans, but not enough like humans to *be* humans. And they were looking at him. Barney had the impression that he was being ordered to stay where he was and wait. But he had the feeling that the humanoids, now descending from the craft, were going to capture him. He ran back toward the safety of the car.

The Hills tried to escape. Betty didn't get far from the car before something grabbed and dragged her into a small clearing in the woods about 150 feet away. The humanoids had already caught Barney and dragged him to the clearing, too. Betty saw her husband next to her and the figures around them. But that was all she could remember.

The next thing they knew, the Hills found themselves driving along a very familiar road and entering their driveway. It was almost dawn. They had no idea where they had been for the previous few hours.

REMINDERS OF WHAT THEY COULD NOT REMEMBER

This would be the beginning of a very revealing inner journey for the Hills. Try as they might, they simply could not return to a normal life.

Barney, who had suffered from hypertension—a disease that finally killed him—continued to be uneasy and had strange symptoms of physical problems. He was unusually worried about his genitals and complained that they pained him. He said his stomach was bothering him, and he was having trouble sleeping at night. Although he tried to remain calm, Barney also seemed to be unusually irritable, as if something were eating at him that he couldn't resolve. Thinking that this was some kind of underlying physical condition, Betty took him to their family doctor. But beyond high blood pressure, the doctor could find nothing wrong with Barney.

While Barney was manifesting physical symptoms, Betty was having serious nightmares. The day after the incident, Betty tried to describe everything to her niece Kathy Marden, but she still could not recall anything that happened between the time of their capture and returning to awareness just as they arrived home. The horrible, repressed memories resurfaced in her dreams.

She may not have been able to retell exactly what happened, but Betty did have proof. The dress she had been wearing that night had pink stains where she remembered the humanoids had touched her. The dress, Barney's symptoms, Betty's nightmares, and the bits and pieces they could remember convinced the Hills that their abduction had not just been a bad dream.

THE LONG ROAD TO THE TRUTH

Betty reported the incident to Pease Air Force Base, near Portsmouth, New Hampshire. An investigator from Pease called her back, interviewed her, and then reported that Betty had probably seen the planet Jupiter. Betty had left out many important details of her encounter, she said years later, because she was afraid the investigator would claim that she was insane. The Hill incident became part of the Air Force's Project Blue Book, the most significant—almost entirely false—official report of the Air Force's investigation of UFOs.

> **HOW TO GET TO EXETER AND PORTSMOUTH BY AIR**
> You can reach the Portsmouth/Exeter area by flying into Manchester-Boston Regional Airport (MHT) in Manchester. You can also fly into Logan International Airport (BOS) in Boston and drive up Route 95 to the Exeter exit.

Barney's doctor could not correlate his patient's repeated complaints of physical ailments with anything physically wrong. He finally suggested that the problem might be emotional issues manifesting themselves as physical symptoms. Upon his doctor's advice, Barney visited a psychiatrist. After only one session in which he learned of Barney's loss of memory, the psychiatrist referred him to Dr. Benjamin Simon, a man who had helped World War II pilots suffering from hysterical symptoms recover lost memories and to confront and integrate the underlying trauma.

Dr. Simon regressed the Hills during separate treatment sessions, recording their responses on tape and through transcription. He instructed both Betty and Barney not to remember what they told him, believing they were not ready to integrate what they told him under hypnosis into their conscious memories. But the stories they told were nevertheless astounding. Separately, Barney and Betty told the same account of their abduction.

> **QUICK FACT**
> Exeter is also home to the Phillips Exeter Academy, one of this country's most highly regarded prep schools.

The Hills said they were placed into a trance-like state by the humanoid creatures and taken from the clearing by force onto what they both described as a craft of some sort. There, the humanoids placed them both under restraint on examination tables and probed and examined them. The Hills could only describe the creatures as aliens from another world. Dr. Simon was shocked by these revelations, but he believed that his patients believed their tale to be true.

Dr. Simon could not ignore that the couple's stories offered matching details from different perspectives. He believed that the Hills had experienced true memory loss. This amnesia seemed to have resulted from some sort of shock, but the Hills claimed that the memory loss was induced.

When the Hills told their separate stories under hypnosis, they both described being placed into a twilight state, taken aboard what seemed like the same craft, and made the subject of painful invasive medical-type examinations. Barney's experience had been particularly embarrassing and painful. The humanoids examined his genitals, creating Barney's concern about his genitals in his post-traumatic waking state. Betty also related to Dr. Simon a medical procedure in which the creatures inserted a thin rod into her abdomen. They sampled fluid in her womb, extracting DNA. These examinations would indicate that the Hills could have been used as test cases for some sort of alien/human cross-fertilization program.

Betty's other exchanges with the extra-terrestrials were more cordial than her husband's. In one instance, an examiner tried to pull out her teeth, but could not; it turned out that it had pulled out Barney's dentures and couldn't understand why Betty's wouldn't come out. Betty tried to explain that some people lose their teeth as they age; the creature asked her to explain aging because it couldn't understand the concept.

> **JOHN FULLER'S JOURNEY FROM PRINT TO FILM**
> Fuller's book about the Hills's abduction was optioned for a television movie of the week. James Earl Jones played Barney and Estelle Parsons portrayed Betty in *Interrupted Journey* (1975).

FACING THE BELIEVING AND UNBELIEVING WORLD

At first, Dr. Simon was very skeptical about the nature of the Hills's encounter, suggesting that Betty's abduction nightmares suggested the same story to Barney, who repeated it under hypnosis. He reported their story as a psychological aberration in a medical journal. But his therapy had helped both Betty and Barney. They had fully integrated their forgotten experiences into their conscious lives and began to speak openly about the event at local UFO meetings. They were interviewed by UFO researchers and investigators and were forthcoming about their stories.

The news of the event gradually leaked out and a reporter for the *Boston Traveler*, John Lutrell, got hold of one of the transcripts of the Hills's regression sessions. He published the story in the *Traveler*, where wire services picked it up and spread word around the country. Betty and Barney suddenly became the center of a publicity firestorm. They did not seek publicity, trying only to figure out what might have happened to them and why, when their private medical sessions became public knowledge. They ultimately told their story to John Fuller, who wrote the book *Interrupted Journey* (1966) about their adventure.

THE HILLS TODAY

Arguments over the veracity of the Hills's story have raged for over forty-five years. Some have suggested that Barney's recollections under hypnosis were simply dreams prompted by an episode of the television show *Outer Limits* that had aired two weeks earlier. In that episode an extraterrestrial with an oversized head and large eyes might have inspired Barney's story. Others have argued that there never was a UFO, only a spotlight on the top of a mountain tower that appeared to be following Barney's car. That

BETTY HILL, YEARS LATER, AT THE ABDUCTION SITE

argument still doesn't explain the Hills's conscious memories of the craft landing and the creatures approaching the car. Some theories rely on the hypnotic session and questions about their legitimacy, but these neglect to acknowledge Betty and Barney's stories told before meeting Dr. Simon.

Over the years other evidence has arisen to support Betty's story. First, the procedure she described where the aliens drew fluid from her abdomen is now known as amniocentesis, a common way to detect birth defects in many pregnancies. Also, the star

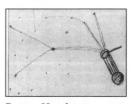

BETTY HILL'S STAR MAP

map that Betty drew under hypnosis turned out to depict a star system known as Zeta Reticuli, a twin-star system not far from our own.

Subsequent findings—not available to either Betty or to astronomers in 1965—have revealed a planetary system in Zeta Reticuli that also appears on the original star map, but not on charts from the 1960s. And finally, Betty's dress—which she preserved after her encounter—was analyzed by organic chemist Dr. Phyllis Budinger and found to have protein remains in the pink stains on the spots where Betty said the creatures grabbed her dress.

The story of the Hills's encounter, although fiercely debated among skeptics and UFO investigators, still stands as one of the most amazing revelations of human encounters with the unknown.

▶ UFO EVENTS

Portsmouth and Exeter are the East Coast's Roswell. Each year, according to the local chamber of commerce and Seacoastonline.com, locals gather to discuss the current cases, new revelations in the Betty and Barney Hill case, and UFO issues in general. Gathering in late winter (usually in February) at the Loaf and Ladle dining room on the shores of the Exeter River, folks talk about the incidents during the year that keep reminding everyone that UFOs are an ongoing phenomenon.

The Exeter UFO Festival takes place every year at the Exeter Town Hall. This event features art contests and craft events, particularly for children. It also holds a writing contest, a costume parade and festival, and a fun adult-supervised event for children called the "UFO Crash Site Safari."

▶ PLACES TO STAY

The Exeter Inn
90 Front Street
Exeter, New Hampshire

The Best Western
137 Portsmouth Avenue
Exeter, New Hampshire

Marriott Fairfield Inn and Suites Portsmouth Exeter
138 Portsmouth Avenue
Exeter, New Hampshire

Inn by the Bandstand
4 Front Street
Exeter, New Hampshire

▶ RESTAURANTS

Loaf and Ladle
9 Water Street
Exeter, New Hampshire

11 Water Street
11 Water Street
Exeter, New Hampshire

Margarita's
93 Portsmouth Avenue
Exeter, New Hampshire

Penang and Tokyo Restaurant
97 Water Street
Exeter, New Hampshire

77 Lafayette Road
Portsmouth, New Hampshire

Revorno Italian Restaurant
149 South Road
Kensington, New Hampshire

CHAPTER TWO
THE PINE BUSH SIGHTINGS

PINE BUSH, NEW YORK

FULL OF HISTORY—AND OF MYSTERY

Located in New York State's Orange County, about two hours north of Manhattan, Pine Bush is a landmark in the history of UFO activity. Like the legends told about nearby Sleepy Hollow and the adventures of the fictional Ichabod Crane, the strange stories of the neighboring towns of Pine Bush and Crawford lingered among the local residents for generations.

Early in the twentieth century, many residents of the area towns wrote about seeing floating balls of light or light energy, sometimes known as "Tesla Balls," after Nikola Tesla, the inventor and engineer who created wireless transmission of electrical energy and who lived in New York.

Stories of glowing orbs in the sky and of strange flying objects that seemed to defy the laws of conventional flight, joined local lore as time passed. No one formally transmitted these stories, and no real archives documented what people saw. Neighbors passed the tales between each other at local events. Mainly *sub rosa* at first, the stories of floating lights began to proliferate during the late 1950s into a true body of lore.

PUTTING PINE BUSH ON THE MAP

Even though story after story came out to support the authenticity of these sightings, residents were not fascinated by the lights: they were downright frightened. And like residents of other areas where strange lights had been observed for years, the Pine Bush inhabitants were circumspect in sharing their observations and fears. Sensational stories too often brought media invasions. They were, however, quite open when talking to legitimate researchers including Ellen Crystall, who spent years in the Pine Bush area tracking down stories and recording the eyewitness accounts.

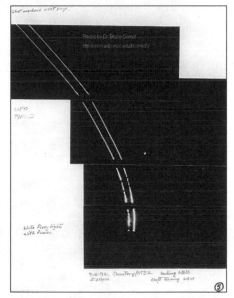

Even without big press leaks, interest in these lights hovering over fields became widespread. By the 1990s, visitors from downstate and UFO investigators from the New York Metropolitan area began making the two-hour jaunt to Orange and Ulster counties just to spend weekends hanging out in fields at night to spot the objects and maybe get a few photographs.

Sky watching in the Pine Bush area became a source for weekend vacations for UFO researchers

BRUCE CORNET'S PHOTO OF LIGHTS OVER THE PINE BUSH AREA

even as open fields in the area disappeared as new construction north of New York City expanded. One would think that with the dwindling areas in which to camp, interest in the Pine Bush sightings would have abated. But it did not. As it turned out, there was more than just lights to see in Pine Bush.

SOMETHING WAS OUT THERE IN THE DARK

As if UFOs weren't enough to wake up a sleepy town, reports from the mid-'90s cite Pine Bush residents' descriptions of phantom beings and shadow creatures in the darkness. Strange animals—ones witnesses claimed could not have been stray dogs or bobcats—dashed across roads and froze in floodlights. People reported hearing strange noises beneath the ground, and rumors began to circulate about spacecraft moving under the earth and underground alien bases. *Something* seemed to be happening underneath the substrata of Ulster and Orange counties.

The rumors, whether based on fact or the frequently retold area lore, inspired more visitors to make the trip to experience and to photograph the goings-on. These visitors only uncovered more mysteries of Pine Bush. Some photographers, who claimed to have seen nothing with their naked eyes, returned home to find out that their photographs had captured floating orbs of different colors.

ORIGINS OF THE ORBS: THE EXPERTS WEIGH IN

Expert opinion hasn't settled the question of the photographed orbs authenticity. Arguments for and against include:

FOR: digital cameras and some film can pick up infrared light—which is normally invisible to the naked eye. The orbs could have been emitting infrared light.

AGAINST: glowing orbs could have just been camera errors. If the picture-takers couldn't see the orbs with their naked eyes, they simply weren't there.

AGAINST: the orbs could just be oversized images of dust or pollen. Small particles can look like a floating orbs set against the background because they float so close to the camera lens that the zoom feature distorts the entire picture.

Despite questions of the sightings' authenticity, thousands of people flocked to the Pine Bush area seeking their own UFOs, orbs, or shadow people. Some talked to local residents who told them stories of alien abductions. During the 1990s, abduction stories were rampant in the UFO community, and books written by researchers and novelists stoked the fires of belief among UFO enthusiasts. Were the stories of alien encounters in areas north of New York City true? It was only a couple of hours' drive and the local hotels and B&Bs were very inviting. Thus, the more popular the stories of the Pine Bush encounters grew, the more people became fascinated and willing to pass along the tales. This was truly a word-of-mouth phenomenon.

THE INFLUENCE OF A LEGEND ON THE LEGEND

The presence of investigator and geologist Bruce Cornet kept the Pine Bush tales churning. He claimed that he was able to photograph strange aerial phenomena and could track beams of light being shot into the sky from underground. Cornet suggested, both in print and on television, that there might be underground spaceships or alien bases in the area beaming signals to spacecraft in orbit. As wild as his ideas sounded to many, others thought they had a truth about them. Dr. Cornet's theories found an audience of researchers anxious to go to Pine Bush.

> **TALES FROM THE TIME**
> Researched works on alien abduction like Budd Hopkins's *Missing Time* (1988) and David Jacobs's *Secret Life* (1992) were popular at the height of the Pine Bush phenomena. Of course, Whitley Strieber's first-hand account played an important role in telling the Pine Bush story to the world.

Cornet's claims of alien contact made his story even more fascinating. He said that he was not only able to track and account for the presence of different life forms, but that these entities contacted him and communicated with him. Reminiscent of tales coming out of the

1950s from such self-described alien contactees as George Adamski, George Van Tassel, and Howard Menger, Cornet's revelations included stories of his being educated by these light beings. They communicated with him telepathically and tried to raise his intellectual grasp of the messages they were sending. Was Cornet one in a long line of anointed prophets and extraterrestrial nuncios bringing a message of hope to people of earth, or was he self-deluded? The evidence could neither rebuff the skeptics nor renounce the believers. The debate itself propelled the fascination with Cornet's message, photographs, and theories of underground UFO facilities in Pine Bush.

MORE FUEL TO THE FIRE

While Cornet's research brought in the die-hard enthusiasts and professionals, one particular Pine Bush resident made the local occurrences a nationwide phenomenon. *Communion*—a 1987 bestselling book and 1989 film directed by Philippe Mora and staring Christopher Walken—tells author Whitley Strieber's first-hand account of being abducted by aliens. Strieber was best known previously for his horror novels-turned-movies like *Wolfen* and *The Hunger*. When he came forward with a fascinating and frightening story of how his Pine Bush cabin became the center of alien visitations and encounters, the masses turned their attention to the seemingly quiet town in New York.

DRIVING DIRECTIONS TO PINE BUSH
For those old enough to remember, Pine Bush sits on Route 52 near the old Route 17, winding north from New Jersey to the resort area of the Catskills. Take Route 17 to the New York State Thruway (I-87) where you will exit at Route 17 and follow the signs for Route 17W. Take 17W to Route 302, where you exit for Pine Bush. Take 302 to Route 52 where you will exit left into the center of Pine Bush.

Strieber's story was chilling: creatures—whether extraterrestrials or entities from another dimension—invaded Strieber's property, confronted the writer and his family, and tampered with their memories of the event. *Communion* and related alien encounter stories in the Pine Bush area helped fuel the already highly charged enthusiasm for the town's proximity to an otherworldly presence.

MORE SIGHTINGS, THEORIES, AND VISITORS

In the second half of the 1990s, stories about a mysterious "face on Mars" also began to circulate on late-night radio talk shows. An image captured by NASA of the Red Planet's surface looked like a human face, inspiring new theories from Bruce Cornet and other experts. Cornet theorized that this new information enabled him to make direct connections to Pine Bush. He claimed that the geography of the Pine Bush area resembled the geography of the area on Mars where people claimed to have observed pyramids and other artificial structures, and that these similarities helped him link the Pine Bush phenomena to the ongoing theories about civilizations on Mars. It would be years before other photos of that area on the Martian surface would reveal that it was no face or structures at all; the images were just a matter of light and shadow.

> **HOW TO GET TO PINE BUSH BY AIR**
> Visitors coming from out of the area can fly into any one of New York's major airports—Newark, La Guardia, and JFK, and drive to Pine Bush via Route 17 in two hours. Travelers can also fly directly into Stewart International Airport (SWF) near Newburgh, New York. From Stewart, take County Road 54 North, to NY State Route 17K west, to County Route 75 North, to Route 52 West (northwest) directly into Pine Bush.

The disconnect might have served to end the Pine Bush fascination, but one dead end couldn't undo a decade of accounts and fresh sightings. When Cornet and his colleagues videotaped a huge black flying triangle against Pine Bush's night sky in 1997, even people who previously had become frustrated with scarce findings began flocking back to the area. They stopped their cars on country roads and camped out alongside private property just to put themselves in the area where they might actually capture a glimpse of a UFO. Many of these visitors were inspired by the recent sightings of similar flying triangles over Phoenix, Arizona. With the same types of craft appearing over the New York suburbs, East Coast enthusiasts found Pine Bush a perfect place to spend a weekend under the stars searching for UFOs and, ideally, catching a glimpse of the entities that navigated them.

PINE BUSH TODAY

By 2000, local authorities began to frown on folks coming up to the area and camping out on private property, but stories of a new Pine Bush phenomenon captured the collective imagination of the UFO community. Bruce Cornet theorized that the area is more than just a UFO hotspot and a possible underground base: it may also be a kind of portal or energy vortex that might function as a gateway between dimensions or worlds. The heightened levels of strange activity, from sightings to abductions, an intense military presence in the area, the proximity to sacred grounds, and a confluence of different types of energy flows: everything pointed to the influence such a portal or vortex would have on the area. Similar arguments have been raised for other historic sites like Stonehenge in the United Kingdom.

WANT MORE FLYING TRIANGLES?
Give Chapters 3, 11, 15, and 16 a read!

Inspired in part by stories from the Skinwalker Ranch in Utah and the legends of mysterious orbs and creatures in the Ozarks's Marley Woods, people were intrigued. Could an interdimensional portal exist so close to New York City? That might explain, people thought, the UFO sightings over northern New Jersey, north and west of the Hudson Valley, and in upper New York State. The people wanted proof.

In 2007, Dr. Cornet took the UFO Hunters to the hundred-year-old cemetery at Beth-El, in the Pine Bush area. They took energy readings to show that the cemetery itself was a kind of energy vortex. The higher the group placed their sensors, the more the readings dropped; the closer to the ground they measured, the higher the readings became. Luckily, the team also brought a ground-penetrating radar unit to determine whether there were any anomalous objects close to the surface. Ultimately, the readings were inconclusive: there might be something metallic under the ground, but it is so deep that it was impossible to get the radar to define its shape or determine its composition. But something *was there*.

The Pine Bush story continues to fascinate UFO researchers. The spectacular photos taken by Cornet and others keep people holding out hope that—at a fortuitous moment along a dark road in Pine Bush—anyone might be able to capture the million-to-one, holy-grail photograph of a UFO.

▶ UFO EVENTS

The local Mutual UFO Network (MUFON) holds meetings, and many locals gather with Hudson Valley UFO research groups, but most visitors hunting for UFOs simply drive the areas outside of Pine Bush and Crawford at night, cameras at-the-ready, looking for aerial phenomena.

Locals have also become inured to the many visitors making their pilgrimages to this UFO hotspot and can direct them to local activities and sky watch outings.

▶ PLACES TO STAY

Harvest Inn Motel
95 Boniface Drive
Pine Bush, New York

Pine Bush House Bed and Breakfast
215 Maple Avenue
Pine Bush, New York

Herman's Erie Hotel
88 Depot Street
Pine Bush, New York

Pine Haven Bed and Breakfast
2781 New Prospect Road
Pine Bush, New York

▶ RESTAURANTS

The Cup and Saucers Diner
82 Boniface Drive
Pine Bush, New York

Golden Steer Manor
66 North Street
Pine Bush, New York

Joey Tomato's
60 Main Street
Pine Bush, New York

Restaurant Repast
72 Main Street
Pine Bush, New York

Antonio's Pizza
2512 Route 52
Pine Bush, New York

Oriental House (Korean/Asian)
78 Main Street
Pine Bush, New York

Pine Bush Chinese Restaurant
2412 Route 52
Pine Bush, New York

Culinary Creations (Sweet Shop)
52 Main Street
Pine Bush, New York

CHAPTER THREE
THE HUDSON VALLEY SIGHTINGS

WORLD EVENTS SET THE STAGE

Even though it is one of the most famous UFO flaps in history, the story of the Hudson Valley sightings doesn't begin in New York. Two prior incidents gained worldwide press and primed the masses for the Hudson Valley happenings.

On December 29, 1980—just a year before the Hudson Valley flap began—three people driving in a car on a lonely road outside Houston, Texas spotted a fiercely bright light floating across the road accompanied by a small formation of U.S. Army Chinook helicopters. The driver, Betty Cash, her friend Vicky Landrum, and Vicky's seven-year-old son Colby, were all irradiated to some degree (probably because Cash stopped and stepped outside to get a better look). Cash ultimately was diagnosed with and died from radiation poisoning. Landrum and little Colby were also burned by the object's intense heat, but survived.

The other event took place on the shores of the North Sea in the United Kingdom at one of the most important nuclear NATO bases operated by the U.S. Air Force. On several successive nights at the end of December 1980, a strange, brightly illuminated object appeared over the nuclear facility and landed in the adjoining Rendlesham

Forest, only to be chased through the woods by an Air Force security personnel detail. The object finally came to rest in a clearing, split into five separate lights, and flew off. Witnesses agreed this was no illusion, fantasy, or New Year's Eve prank. The testimony given at a National Press Club press conference in November 2007 confirmed that the object was real, palpable to the touch, and seemingly intelligently guided. It also left landing skid impressions in the wet dirt in the forest and significant radiation residue at its landing spot. Moreover, one of the witnesses said he actually touched the object that landed and said it had strange markings on it that he copied into his notebook.

HOW TO GET TO THE HUDSON VALLEY BY TRAIN OR PLANE
The Metro North and Amtrak from New York's Grand Central Station make stops at all the river towns. Air travelers headed to the northern towns in the valley will fly into Stewart International Airport (SWF) near Newburgh and drive about forty minutes to the Kingston/Rhinebeck area. Newark or La Guardia Airports are fine arrival points for towns further south.

The British and American military intelligence services tried to come to grasp with the apparent truth: an otherworldly event of great magnitude had occurred on a base storing nuclear weapons. Public awareness of the possibilities rose up on both sides of the Atlantic. It was against this background that residents of the Hudson Valley first saw the configurations of colored lights in December 1981.

THE FAMOUS FLAP BEGINS

The Hudson Valley sightings began in Kent, New York on New Year's Eve, 1981. A former police officer saw a formation of lights floating through the southern sky from his backyard. At first—as is typical of most witnesses—he believed the lights were the navigation lights of one or more airplanes.

But as the lights approached, the witness realized he should have heard the unmistakable whine of engines or the roar of jets, even if they were thousands of feet above him. Yet there was nothing but silence. Then as the lights came closer, the witness realized that the lights didn't move independently. He could even see enough of an outline to confirm that it was a single craft. The structure was shaped like a triangle, perhaps with softly rounded edges and a distinctive body. As the object passed almost overhead, it emitted something like a soft electrical hum, as if it had a pulsating electric engine. It didn't sizzle, like an arcing current; rather, it sounded like something was generating a powerful field that throbbed with each surge of energy.

A CONSENSUS

Over the next two years, even before claims of hoaxes filled the newspapers and airwaves, witnesses saw the same type of craft traveling up and down the Hudson Valley and across the river to Connecticut. This UFO—whether extraterrestrial or a new Air Force craft—would also appear regularly over the west side of Manhattan, Phoenix, Arizona, and parts of Nevada.

Most witnesses assume they're seeing a giant plane when they see these types of dark triangular shapes against the night sky. However, because the triangles are silent as they sweep across the witnesses' fields of vision and because they are so large, people begin to doubt what it is they're seeing. They perceive that the object moves very slowly, hovering or floating through the sky. The smooth and unhurried

THE HUDSON VALLEY
The Hudson Valley is one of New York State's most historic regions. Stretching from Westchester, just north of New York City, to the state capital at Albany, the Hudson Valley is not only one of the most scenic areas in the Northeast, it probably boasts the most attractions and tourist sites in the region as well.

movement belies the notion that a plane is passing overhead. Even if a technology that muffles the sound of the jet engines exists, jets simply don't hover. Nor do prop-driven planes. Any kind of plane has to fly at a certain velocity above stall-speed lest they lose the force of lift and drop out of the sky. Dirigibles and balloons can seem to float along, but unless they have their own propulsion system to drive them forward, they drift on the upper currents. And though helicopters' rotors fight currents, their throbbing whirr is unmistakable. The first witness and the thousands of others who followed him agreed: this was neither a conventional aircraft, nor a balloon, nor a helicopter. It was a flying triangle.

BRINGING IN THE CAVALRY

These ongoing reports of sightings were shared informally among friends and neighbors, transmitted to 911 dispatchers, and appeared regularly in local newspapers. The buzz grew until it finally prompted local UFO researchers to seek investigative help from national sources. Among those who became curious in the reports of such consistent mass sightings was Dr. J. Allen Hynek, the astronomer who had been the official skeptic/advisor to the U.S. Air Force's Project Blue Book before it was disbanded in 1969. Hynek, once freed from his official role as the skeptic, then came forward with a change of perspective and a whistle to blow. He became an advocate of UFO research and sought explanations for just the type of incidents that folks in the Hudson Valley were reporting.

A SCENIC DRIVE
A drive along the routes connecting the Hudson River towns made famous by the flap is almost a weekend vacation in itself, particularly in October when the whether is still pleasant and the leaves have begun to turn.

Working with researcher Phil Imbrogno— with whom he and Bob Pratt wrote the book *Night Siege* (1987) about the Hudson Valley sightings—Hynek encouraged local researchers to collect as many sighting reports as they could. Hundreds of reports—sometimes numbering well over 200 a night— described the same object. The researchers were able to make better

THE SCOOP ON PROJECT BLUE BOOK

The Air Force's investigations into UFO reports began in the late 1940s and were known by the names Project Sign and Project Grudge before the final codename, Project Blue Book, was created in 1952. Blue Book, at first thought to be the military's honest attempt to compile and investigate UFO sightings, was eventually determined to be a simple cover-up mission. It debunked most sightings and spirited away the most troubling reports into more secret files before being shut down in 1969.

sense of the object and the ongoing sightings thanks to the number of witnesses. They felt that the hundreds of people who believed they saw something in the sky couldn't *all* be deceiving themselves.

Ironically, on one of the very same nights in March 1983, that the researchers were at work on compiling the data, motorists driving along the Taconic State Parkway became part of the flap. It was a famous group sighting, reminiscent of the scene from the movie *Close Encounters of the Third Kind* (1977). Drivers pulled their cars over to the shoulder of the road and watched in awe as the huge object noiselessly floated over them. The 911 switchboards lit up with so many calls that night that the dispatchers were overwhelmed. If there *had* been a true emergency there may not have been enough open lines to handle both the emergency and the sighting.

QUICK FACT
Few people realize that Hynek was *also* an advisor to the producers of *Close Encounters of the Third Kind*.

THE INCIDENT AT INDIAN POINT

Hudson Valley sightings weren't all excitement and no fear. The drama and threat peaked when the giant flying triangle appeared over the Indian Point nuclear power plant on two separate occasions in 1984.

Not only did the triangle appear in the middle of the ongoing flap, but the motion picture *China Syndrome* and the release of radioactive contaminated water at the Three Mile Island had already put the East Coast in a panic over nuclear accidents. It's no surprise, then, that the strange craft reportedly hovering over a nuclear power plant just north of New York City was a major incident in itself.

But as terrifying as the sighting was, witnesses willing to talk were hard to come by. Then *UFO Magazine* former editor-in-chief Vicky Cooper had to report the event based on interviews with sources who refused to be named for fear of their jobs and reputations. But under the mask of anonymity, the truth was as shocking as any movie.

According to *UFO Magazine*, the two appearances occurred just ten days apart. The first one, on June 14, amounted only to a sighting by security officers as the craft flew over the plant. In light of the second, more extensive UFO event, this first fly-over might have been

A STRING OF LIGHTS, PURPORTEDLY OVER THE HUDSON VALLEY AREA OF NEW YORK

simply for surveillance purposes. On June 24 one of the security guards who noticed the large triangle approaching the plant yelled out: "Here comes that UFO again!" He alerted the other guards as the craft hovered about 300 feet over Reactor 3, the only reactor online that evening. The craft was massive; the guards estimated that it spanned 1,000 feet. It spent at least ten, long minutes over the active reactor. Suspicious of the time the craft spent hovering at low altitudes, some of the management personnel considered calling in the Air National Guard or the Air Force to confront the object.

Some investigators accounted for the object's appearance and flight by dismissing it as a blimp. But a *thousand-foot* blimp intruding over restricted airspace and staying there for no other purpose than to draw attention seems very unlikely. Just to make sure, researchers after the event contacted facilities that handled blimps and large balloons: none of them reported having any craft in the air that night. Moreover, the shape of the craft itself—the flying V now familiar to the Valley—wasn't like any conventional blimp anyone had ever seen before. The craft was clearly a mystery.

Night Siege coauthor Phil Imbrogno said that after the UFO incident, a crack developed in Reactor 3. Further, Imbrogno has said that the UFO appearances continued over Indian Point even after the July 24 incident. New York Power Authority spokesman Carl Patrick denies both claims and has said that—despite accounts to the contrary—there were no fluctuations in power at the plant, the security system was not disabled, and no upgrades to the security system were installed after

ATTRACTIONS IN THE HUDSON VALLEY COMMUNITIES

Visitors to the Hudson Valley can also avail themselves of community attractions such as the local museums and community centers. They not only have a cultural appeal, but they are also fascinating for families with children and for grownups who still harbor childhood fantasies of iconic Americana.

The Trolley Museum
89 East Strand Street
Kingston, New York

The FASNY Museum of Firefighting
117 Harry Howard Avenue
Hudson, New York

The Hudson River Maritime Museum
50 Roundout Landing
Kingston, New York

Hudson Highland Cruises
6 Columbus Avenue
Cornwall-on Hudson, New York

The Old Rhinebeck Aerodrome
9 Norton Road
Rhinebeck, New York

Museum Village
1010 Route 17M
Monroe, New York

Sugar Loaf Art & Craft Village
1371 Kings Highway
Chester, New York

United States Military Academy
West Point, New York

the incident. Records from the Nuclear Regulatory Commission also do not show any irregularities in the plant's operation, but UFO researchers who've spent years searching government records and interviewing government spokespersons say that when it comes to talking about UFOs, government people simply deny, deny, and deny. It's no wonder Indian Point researchers hit dead ends, too.

MORE TRUTHS TO SHARE

By 1987, residents of the Hudson Valley had filed so many reports of UFO sightings that it was clear that no formation of planes could account for all of it. In fact, many of the residents had come to believe that their area was the object of some kind of nonhuman surveillance. To collect data and bring many of the witnesses together, Phil Imbrogno and New York attorney Peter Gersten held a conference, also attended by the author of *Communion*, Whitley Strieber; alien abduction researcher and author Budd Hopkins; and Pine Bush investigator Ellen Crystall. At the conference, some of the witnesses revealed more than sightings. Many reported actual abductions, telepathic communication with an intelligence aboard the craft, and actual face-to-face meetings with alien life forms. These were incredible accounts indicating that, if true, the Hudson Valley sightings were far broader in scope than they were first assumed to be.

EVEN THE "LIKELY EXPLANATION" CAN'T BE TRUE

The overwhelming number of witnesses weren't enough to convince some people, though. A group of pilots, calling themselves the Stormville Flyers, went as far as *taking credit* for the early 1980s Hudson Valley sightings. They claimed to have flown routes over the Hudson Valley in tight formations so as to give the impression of a single craft sporting a V-shaped formation of lights. They also said they were able to change the colors of the lights as they were flying, accounting for exactly what some observers said they saw. And they said that they were able to fly so proficiently in a tight formation that when they turned off their lights it seemed that the craft disappeared. As for the hovering nature of the craft: the pilots' claim that they were flying at such low speeds that from a distance it looked as if the craft was creeping along. And the humming sound? It was the sound of their propeller engines cruising at low speed.

For the Stormville Flyers to have been responsible for every sighting, it would mean that even experienced pilots on the ground (who were among the witnesses) and police officers (who are generally excellent observers) would have been consistently fooled by the formation of planes for a number of years. Moreover, the Stormville Flyers's story does not explain the incident at Indian Point. In addition, as happy-go-lucky as these "bored" private pilots might have been, it is a very rare private pilot reckless enough to chance flying over the restricted airspace of a nuclear power reactor and risk interception by the Air National Guard. Bored pilots are not *so* bored that they want to trade their pilots' licenses for time in federal custody.

WHAT IS IT WITH UFOS AND NUCLEAR FACILITIES?
RAF Bentwaters, Suffolk, England, the site of a 1980 UFO incident, was a nuclear weapons base and stored nukes for use by forward squadrons of NATO and U.S. Air Force warplanes in Germany. The famous 1947 Roswell incident involved Walker Field, the first Strategic Air Command facility where nuclear weapons would be stored and the base that loaded the atomic bomb onto the B-29 that dropped it over Hiroshima to end World War II.

A RETORT FROM THE BELIEVERS

Most of the UFO researchers investigating the Hudson Valley sightings have agreed that the Stormville Flyers were not solely responsible for the flap. At best, they concede, private pilots may have been responsible for *some* of the sightings. And certainly other people, influenced by reports in the newspapers and on television, might have duped themselves into believing that they were witnesses as well. In fact, at the Hudson Valley Sighting conference, investigators discounted the majority of the reports as explainable by other means. A core minority of consistent reports defied explanation by conventional means.

It is also unlikely that a respected scholar and U.S. government analyst like J. Allen Hynek would have become involved in investigating a phenomenon that could have been explained away so conventionally. Wouldn't have reports from local airfields, searching for flight plans, and talking to witnesses at least put Hynek and Imbrogno on alert that this could have been a hoax from the beginning?

The claims of the Hudson Valley sightings' veracity, then, hold firm in the face of doubt. The researchers had quite a bit to work with in this case. The sightings of triangular craft stretched across three states and nine years. Beyond the valley in New York, local residents spotted the craft from country routes in Connecticut. There were also accompanying sightings in the late 1980s in northern New Jersey on the western side of the Hudson River and even one report from the West Side Highway in Manhattan. Together these continuing sightings amounted to one of the longest UFO flaps in the history of American ufology. According to some researchers, the flying triangle sightings are still going on today, although they are no longer in the headlines.

As in all UFO investigations, after they methodically eliminate as many conventional explanations as they can, investigators can only conclude that the object remains unidentified. Even when a probable solution is offered—like the story of the Stormville Flyers—the witnesses who are unable to identify what they saw often just want confirmation that the object was *truly* unidentifiable. And that was the point of the investigation in the first place.

▶ UFO EVENTS

Actual UFO conferences, talks, and meetings—many of them hosted and attended by the Hudson Valley original investigators Budd Hopkins and Phil Imbrogno—take place in New York City itself. Among these conferences are:

- The Budd Hopkins Intruders' Foundation Seminars
- The Disclosure Network/New York meets on the first Sunday of every month.
- The Culture of Contact, held in New York City or New Jersey on a yearly basis.
- The UFO Roundtable in Yonkers. This is hosted by Paul Greco and takes place on the first Wednesday of every month.

▶ PLACES TO STAY

The Hudson Valley itself is a string of tourist-oriented villages and towns along the Hudson River stretching from the area north of Westchester County all the way to Albany. Along the way, there are many historic bed and breakfasts, which folks can find by searching their favorite sites when planning the trip. Some inexpensive and convenient options in the Kingston/Rhinebeck area include:

Rodeway Inn
239 Forest Hill Drive, Route 28 West
Kingston, New York

Hampton Inn
1307 Ulster Avenue
Kingston, New York

Super 8
487 Washington Avenue
Kingston, New York

Quality Inn & Suites
114 Route 28
Kingston, New York

Marriott Courtyard, Kingston
500 Frank Sottile Boulevard
Kingston, New York

Rhinecliff Hotel
4 Grinnell Street
Rhinecliff, New York

Whistle Wood Farm Bed and Breakfast
52 Pells Road
Rhinebeck, New York

Delamater Inn and Conference Center
25 Garden Street
Rhinebeck, New York

▶ PLACES TO STAY—continued

Rhinebeck Village Inn
6260 Route 9
Rhinebeck, New York

The Copper Penny Inn
2406 New Hackensack Road
Poughkeepsie, New York

The Looking Glass Bed and Breakfast
30 Chestnut Street
Rhinebeck, New York

▶ RESTAURANTS

Perhaps the best guide to restaurants in the Hudson Valley can be found in the *Hudson Valley Magazine*, particularly the March food and dining issue each year. A quick look at the magazine's website at *www.hvmag.com* will provide a complete list of restaurants in the valley organized by type of cuisine and including restaurant locations and phone numbers. The Hudson Valley restaurants also sponsor the Hudson Valley Restaurant Week in March when lunches are prix fixe at $20 and dinner at $28. Participating restaurants, locations, and the types of cuisine they serve can all be found at *www.hudsonvalleyrestaurantweek.com*.

Andy's Place
45 Dutchess Avenue
Poughkeepsie, New York

Blue Plate
1 Kinderhook Street
Chatham, New York

Another Fork in the Road
1215 Route 199
Milan, New York

McKinney & Doyle
10 Charles Colman Boulevard
Pawling, New York

Bacchus
4 South Chestnut Street
New Paltz, New York

Cheryl's Fried Fish & Soul Food
24 East Main Street
Middletown, New York

Beebs
30 Plank Road
Newburgh, New York

Armadillo Bar & Grill
97 Abeel Street
Kingston, New York

▶ RESTAURANTS—continued

Ship to Shore
15 West Strand Street
Kingston, New York

Sapore
1108 Main Street
Fishkill, New York

Arielle
51 East Market Street
Rhinebeck, New York

Buffet de la Gare
155 Southside Avenue
Hastings-on-Hudson, New York

Bavarian Manor Country Inn
866 Mountain Avenue
Purling, New York

Jaipore Royal Indian
280 Route 22
Brewster, New York

China Rose
1 Shatzell Avenue
Rhinecliff, New York

Sukhothai
516 Main Street
Beacon, New York

Yobo Restaurant
Route 300
Newburgh, New York

NY Firehouse Grille
50 Welcher Avenue
Peekskill, New York

12 Grapes
12 North Division Street
Peekskill, New York

Zephs'
638 Central Avenue
Peekskill, New York

Taormina II Restaurant
59 Hudson Avenue
Peekskill, New York

CHAPTER FOUR
THE BUCKS COUNTY SIGHTINGS

BUCKS COUNTY, PENNSYLVANIA AND MERCER AND
HUNTERDON COUNTIES, NEW JERSEY

MANY SIGHTINGS, ONE NAME

The mass UFO sightings in 2008 may be called the Bucks County flap, but the reports came in from all across the state, from Pittsburgh to the shores of the Delaware River and east across the Delaware Valley into New Jersey. The chief investigator of the incident, Mutual UFO Network (MUFON) state director John Ventre, called it one of the most important UFO incidents of the decade, ranking with the world famous Stephenville, Texas, and Phoenix, Arizona sightings.

The fascinating series of incidents put historic and quiet Bucks County, Pennsylvania in the center of ongoing media and research interest. The first sighting in the flap was reported in January 2008. Three more months worth of sightings made local, state, and national news: witnesses saw star-like objects over their backyards, from shopping center parking lots, and over Route 1. Locals' stories were featured on a Discovery Channel series and were revisited in an episode of *UFO Hunters* on the History Channel.

MUFON state investigator Bob Gardner—who had covered many UFO sightings before the 2008 flap—personally interviewed scores of witnesses to compare the details and plot the courses and trajectories of the objects. Official UFO reports logged 130 sightings across Pennsylvania in 2008, 127 more than the year before.

This was a UFO flap that the media didn't walk away from or treat derisively. The local media was very aggressive in following this story. Print and broadcast reporters, including some from Philadelphia-area affiliates of the major news networks, interviewed Ventre and Gardner extensively. The sightings in the Delaware Valley were so extensive, coming in night after night, that the stories quickly made national news as well. And with the media coverage, even local residents who *had* seen some

HOW TO GET TO THE BUCKS COUNTY AREA BY AIR
If you plan to fly into the Bucks County and Lambertville areas, book your tickets into Philadelphia International Airport (PHL). From there, you can reach Bucks County, Lambertville, and Princeton by car.

of the lights were quick to provide news agencies with explanations for the events that seemed more reasonable than a UFO flap. But when compared to the reports and claims witnesses continued to make, the conventional explanations made no sense.

THE SENSIBLE ANSWERS JUST DON'T MAKE SENSE

Some residents claimed that the UFOs and the lights were really just candles affixed to balloons. But the MUFON investigators said that the proliferation of sightings and reports from different places at almost the same time meant that either there were scores of hoaxers coordinating launches via cell phone, or that at least some of the sightings were not balloons at all.

Investigators reported that many of the witnesses said they saw the lights hover in place. Balloons, Ventre suggested in a report, don't hover motionless when the winds aloft were even only a couple of miles an hour. Balloons float with the wind or at the very least rise; they just do not remain stationary in the upper air. Therefore, the balloon explanation for the recorded sightings simply doesn't comport with the statements that the witnesses gave investigators.

GOING ON THE RECORD

Ventre's MUFON report is the authoritative record of the Bucks County sightings. These stories are among many others from across the region.

MARCH 28, 2008, 10:20 P.M.
HATBORO, MONTGOMERY COUNTY, PENNSYLVANIA

A man was walking his dog when he noticed an aircraft heading southwest at an extreme height. Not long afterwards, four other, unusual looking shapes flew low, heading east, without any noise. Each had at least one red light on top and flashing and static lights elsewhere. None of them followed any of the normal flight patterns for aircraft in the area. They headed east, swerved north, and started to fly away. The witness immediately returned home and mentioned the sighting to his wife. He looked out a window only to see the crafts circling again. He called his wife to come look. She confirmed that the strange aircraft were flying in a circle, again with no noise. Even their son agreed that that they appeared unusual, giving the appearance of quick-moving helicopters but without the familiar pulse of rotors. The witnesses reported that the crafts seemed to be searching for something, but no searchlights were used.

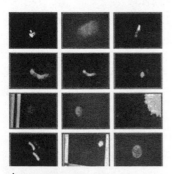

A MONTAGE OF ORBS PHOTOGRAPHED ACROSS THE PENNSYLVANIA AND NEW JERSEY COUNTRYSIDE

After about fifteen minutes the aircraft flew off to the northwest. Several minutes later, the family heard several airplanes overhead. They all went to the windows, and sure enough *these* aircraft were behaving as any earthly planes do.

The family of witnesses was convinced, thanks to the opportunity to
see both types of aircraft, that the first set was nothing like the conventional airplanes or helicopters we see every day.

JUNE 3, 2008, AT 4:20 A.M.
DOYLESTOWN, BUCKS COUNTY, PENNSYLVANIA

Early in the morning, the witness awoke, looked out his window,
and saw what he at first believed to be a small cloud heading his way.
This witness told MUFON field investigator Elise Simon that the closer

THINGS TO DO AND SEE NEAR BUCKS COUNTY

Like New York's Lower Hudson Valley, the Bucks County area is close to two
major metropolitan areas, making it perfect for a weekend trip to the area's UFO
conferences, local farm stands, and family attractions.

New Hope, Pennsylvania and Lambertville, New Jersey—twin cities on either
side of the Delaware—are known for art, antiques, eighteenth- and nineteenth-
century house tours, repertory theater, and some of the best local hotels and
restaurants within a two-hour drive of New York City.

And just a half-hour to the east is Princeton, New Jersey, another small city
known for its hotels, restaurants, shopping, and Ivy League atmosphere.
Princeton is an absolute mix of academia, high-tech and old-time corporate, and
houses right out of the 1700s.

Heading north up the Delaware River from New Hope and Lambertville is the picturesque town of Stockton, New Jersey. Visitors can stay at the famous Stockton
Inn, the "small hotel" with a wishing well that Richard Rogers and Lorenz Hart
referred to in the Broadway musical *On Your Toes* and the movie *Pal Joey*.

Just a few miles up-river from Stockton is the literary enclave of Lumberville,
Pennsylvania, where Julia Child once lived. Further north are the very quaint
communities of Erwinna and Upper Black Eddy.

the cloud got to his house, the more he realized that it didn't look like a cloud at all. It took on the shape of an "elongated hexagon" that had a color darker than the pre-dawn sky. The witness estimated that the object was floating about 600 feet above the ground and was about 100 feet long and 100 feet wide with "two sides longer on either side." The object circled his property at a slow speed and then came back for another pass. No noise came from the object: not the roar of jets, not a hum, not a hiss. Then it climbed to a higher altitude and disappeared.

> **QUICK FACT**
> The Bucks County, Lambertville, and Princeton areas are known for more than excellent UFO hunting. The area also has wonderful antique hunting opportunities!

The object returned for another flyover of the witness's property on July 27 at 4:05 A.M., according to field investigator Simon and investigator Bob Gardner. This time the witness got a closer look. He could clearly see that it was not a single craft in a hexagonal shape, but six craft connected to one another and to what he called a "mother ship," a seventh shape with elongated protruding sides and what appeared to be windows running alongside.

MUFON investigators Ventre and Gardner sought information from the air traffic control tower at the Philadelphia International Airport about objects that appeared on the radar that night. The airport confirmed that they found a large object on radar in the same position as the Doylestown witness's sighting at around 4:30 A.M., but that the object had no transponder transmitting.

JUNE 25, 2008, AT 1:00 A.M.
LEVITTOWN, BUCKS COUNTY, PENNSYLVANIA

A witness saw a boomerang-shaped object with white lights along the tips flying slowly at an altitude of about 1,000 feet. He heard a low rumbling sound, not at all like the sound of a jet engine. The object, according to the witness's description, had colored lights at the rear and along the sides. He watched the object fly slowly overhead for about five minutes.

JULY 16, 2008, AT 11:45 A.M.
PHILADELPHIA, PHILADELPHIA COUNTY, PENNSYLVANIA

A witness driving home from work saw an H-shaped object over her car. It hovered for a while and then disappeared behind a tree line. When she returned home, she asked her husband whether he had noticed any Philadelphia police helicopters around their house. He said that he had not seen helicopters at all. The object the witness saw emitted no noise, flew very slowly, and reminded her of a Star Wars X-fighter.

AUGUST 3, 2008, AT 10:10 P.M.
PHILADELPHIA, PHILADELPHIA COUNTY, PENNSYLVANIA

A witness sitting on his balcony heard a strange humming sound in his ear just before he spotted a bright ball of light traveling across the sky from west to east. Because he lives near the Philadelphia International Airport, he immediately checked the sky to see if any planes were in a holding pattern or taking off. But he couldn't see any traffic over the airport. The bright light heading across the sky kept moving slowly until it faded from view.

Earlier on that same day, other witnesses saw a bright ball of light from the New Jersey side of the Delaware River in Deptford, a town directly across the river from Philadelphia. Witnesses also saw a similar object that same day in West Virginia and in Michigan.

JULY 8, 2008, AT 4:10 A.M.
LEVITTOWN, BUCKS COUNTY, PENNSYLVANIA

Perhaps one of the most interesting Bucks County sightings—and one that made it to the *UFO Hunters* episode covering the flap—

ultimately turned into a close encounter of the third kind. The witness was out in the yard with her dog early in the morning. She had seen anomalous lights in the sky on previous occasions during the early part of 2008, but this time was different. The lights she saw that morning reminded her of a face: "three that looked like two eyes and a nose." She perceived these as headlights. Further out in front of the object, she could see a fourth, pink colored light.

The craft was flying at a low altitude as if it were looking for something or scanning the area. The witness said it was "skipping" or "shuttering" as it moved. According to her statement in the MUFON report, it emitted a "blue fog out of the back, which contained silver flakes falling down into the tree tops and filtering down through the trees till they hovered about three feet off the ground." The flakes enveloped part of a tree in the witness's backyard, making it shimmer as if objects were swirling around it. Then, the object seemed to suck the flakes and beam away.

ON THE ROAD TO THE BUCKS COUNTY AREA
- From Philadelphia International Airport to New Hope: 50 miles
- From Newark Airport to Princeton: 40 miles
- From Boston to Lambertville, New Jersey: 280 miles
- From Boston, New York, and Northern New Jersey, take I-95 South to the Princeton exit, Trenton exit, or New Hope exit. From Philadelphia, take I-95 North to New Hope, Trenton, or Princeton.

The witness observed the whole encounter for what she thought was about forty minutes. But when she went back into the house, she realized that she had been watching the event unfold for over an hour. Her encounter not only involved an interaction between the witness and the craft, but the phenomenon of "missing time," the passage of time that could not be accounted for by a witness. Strangely, perhaps in conjunction or as a result of the witness's misperception of the passage of time, a robin was found dead on the patio the next morning. It had been living happily for four months in a tree—the same tree that had been covered with the suspect flakes the night before. What could have caused that robin's death? Was it something in the metallic sprinkles that the witness described or was it the effects of the beam on the tree and the robin living in it?

Fortunately, investigator Bob Gardner retrieved samples from the scene and discovered trace evidence. Gardner and John Ventre sent the samples of soil and leaves to the well-respected scientists at BLT Research for an evaluation. BLT's founder Professor W. C. Levengood, a biophysicist, discovered that the leaves had been subjected to high heat or radiation causing a chemical reaction in which the substance anthocyanin appeared. Moreover, the leaves looked as if they had aged three or four months so that they were dry and brittle, as if they were dying, and had actually changed shape. Might this have accounted for the death of the robin as well?

Further research at BLT indicated that the leaf samples had boron and magnesium on their surface. Boron is used in advanced "stealth" fighter jets because it does not reflect radar pings; its presence in the leaves was suspect for sure. The magnesium is much more common and is used in phosphorescent devices like fireworks. The witness explained that the family *had* set off fireworks in her backyard, but there was no presence of magnesium in the control soil samples the MUFON field investigators retrieved from the scene. If the fireworks hadn't emitted enough magnesium to affect the soil, they wouldn't have affected the leaves either.

This witness was not the only person to have observed the beam emanating from the craft. Another witness ten miles away also saw the beam and the snowflake-like effect inside the beam.

AUTHORITATIVE CONFIRMATION

The Bucks County flap was one of the most intriguing recent UFO mass sightings. The witnesses did not communicate with each other and did not know each other. Some of the sightings were also backed up by the local police who responded to reports of strange lights in the sky. The FAA radar at the Philadelphia airport also corroborates sightings in the city. And the trace evidence left at the Levittown scene, even though not conclusive, did turn up the presence of chemicals on the samples not present in the control samples. Even though no definitive evidence proves that these objects were extraterrestrial craft, the reports establish that *something* strange was going on in the area.

▶ UFO EVENTS

The Pennsylvania MUFON hosts annual gatherings across the state for ufologists interested in the Bucks County flap. In October 2010, a Bucks County conference was held at the local Sheraton hotel. A second conference in the western part of the state, just outside of Pittsburgh at Westmoreland Community College, was held just a few weeks later. Past conferences have also been held in Philadelphia. The agendas include not just the latest UFO sightings, but personal stories of alien abductions, reports on recovered UFO trace evidence, theories concerning the origin of UFOs and alien contact, and even research from the hunt for Big Foot in rural areas of Pennsylvania. Visitors can find details on MUFON state director John Ventre's personal website at *www.johnventre.com/Conference.html*.

▶ PLACES TO STAY

As the area is convenient to New York City, Philadelphia, and Princeton, New Jersey, there is a wide range of familiar franchised hotels from Marriotts to Holiday Inns, all of which can be contacted via their central reservation numbers. But some visitors may prefer the charm of the many locally owned bed-and-breakfasts, historic hotels, and colonial taverns. These are some of the very special places to stay that are well worth a weekend in the country while looking for UFOs and attending a UFO conference:

The Nassau Inn
10 Palmer Square
Princeton, New Jersey

The Inn at Glencairn
3301 Lawrenceville Road
Princeton, New Jersey

Stockton Inn
1 Main Street
Stockton, New Jersey

The York Street House Bed & Breakfast
42 York Street
Lambertville, New Jersey

The Black Bass Hotel
3774 River Road
Lumberville, Pennsylvania

The 1740 House Inn
3690 River Road
Lumberville, Pennsylvania

Centre Bridge Inn
2998 North River Road
New Hope, Pennsylvania

The Inn at Phillips Mill
2590 River Road
New Hope, Pennsylvania

▶ PLACES TO STAY—continued

Logan Inn
10 West Ferry Street
New Hope, Pennsylvania

The Mansion Inn
9 South Main Street
New Hope, Pennsylvania

The Wedgwood Inn
11 West Bridge Street
New Hope, Pennsylvania

The Hotel du Village
2535 River Road
New Hope, Pennsylvania

The Fox and Hound
246 West Bridge Street
New Hope, Pennsylvania

▶ RESTAURANTS

Lahiere's
5-11 Witherspoon Street
Princeton, New Jersey

The Alchemist and Barrister
28 Witherspoon Street
Princeton, New Jersey

The Bent Spoon
35 Palmer Square West
Princeton, New Jersey

Chuck's Spring Street Café
16 Spring Street
Princeton, New Jersey

The Lambertville Station
11 Bridge Street
Lambertville, New Jersey

Manon Restaurant
19 North Union Street
Lambertville, New Jersey

Anton's at the Swan
43 South Main Street
Lambertville, New Jersey

Rojo's Café
243 N. Union Street #10
Lambertville, New Jersey

Martine's River House
14 East Ferry Street
New Hope, Pennsylvania

Marsha Brown
15 South Main Street
New Hope, Pennsylvania

Havana Restaurant
105 South Main Street
New Hope, Pennsylvania

Mother's
34 North Main Street
New Hope, Pennsylvania

The Landing
22 North Main Street
New Hope, Pennsylvania

CHAPTER FIVE
THE KECKSBURG INCIDENT: ALIEN CRASH OR A NAZI TIME MACHINE LANDING?

KECKSBURG, PENNSYLVANIA

INCOMING!

In the chill of a December evening in 1965, unbeknownst to people living in the Midwest and in western Pennsylvania, civilian and military radars tracked an incoming object heading south across Canada. Silently, but in what looked like a controlled descent, the object crossed the Canadian border, flew over Michigan and Ohio, and made a long sweeping S-curve as it approached Pittsburgh, Pennsylvania.

By then it was visible to residents just getting home from work or sitting down to dinner. But it was not just another anomalous or odd sight: it looked like a flaming meteor screaming in for a crash. The panic was palpable. For those who'd seen the 1956 movie *War of the Worlds* or heard Orson Welles's 1938 radio broadcast of the H.G. Wells story, this was *exactly* how the Martians landed.

FIRST ON THE CRASH SITE

A Greensburg radio station reporter named John Murphy took the first call from a female witness a little after 6:30 P.M. The caller described a bright, burning star falling over Greensburg, the town neighboring

Kecksburg. She and her children followed the trail of the falling object to a site in a rural area inside the municipal limits of Kecksburg. They found a deep gouge in the earth, cut by the object skidding to a halt. They couldn't see anything up close due to the smoke, but the caller was able to find high enough ground to look down into the trench.

The violet-blue object was still glowing and burning and smoking. The trench, too, looked like it was hot and singed by the impact. She told Murphy it looked like a "four-pointed star." Murphy, probably thinking it was an aircraft that had gone down, notified the Pennsylvania State Troopers. The state police immediately dispatched a unit to the location to meet up with the witness. Murphy himself hurried to the crash site. For a local news radio station, an airplane crash in town was big news and a live report would have been invaluable publicity.

And that was only the first witness's story.

FLOCKING TO THE SCENE

Billy Bulebush, a local resident, was tinkering with his 1962 Chevy Corvair in his garage when he looked up at a light shining over his shoulder and saw the object speeding past overhead. He remembered that it had seemed especially dark that December evening, and the light flooding into his garage was by no means normal. He jumped into his car and drove off after the falling object.

By the time the state police detail arrived, fascinated onlookers like Bulebush had followed the burning trail in the sky and were standing on a small rise staring down into the ditch at the glowing object. What was it? Almost all the witnesses agreed that it was an acorn- or bell-shaped object, even something looking like a ten- or eleven-foot-long artillery shell. One witness who got especially close to the object said that it was shaped like a beehive and that it had a band around its base on which he could make out strange designs almost like hieroglyphics. It was not like any lettering he had ever seen before.

The state police moved the small crowd back from the glowing object. Anyone could see that it certainly was not a plane, so the troopers called in the military. To everyone's surprise, the military were already on their way. Trucks, troop carriers, and a flatbed arrived and took control. The soldiers were armed and pushed the crowd and the state troopers back from the impact area.

Vince Lobeck, a local resident and truck driver, got a particularly close look at the object and the inscription across it. While most of the onlookers hung back, Lobeck made his way down the slope and approached the glowing "acorn," taking special notice of the band along its base. Though he couldn't place the markings, he described them as "ancient writing." The object didn't emanate any heat, but there seemed to be a haze around it that made it shimmer in the damp darkness. Lobeck said he was tempted to touch it, but something in the back of his mind told him not to get any closer than ten feet. He said that the object had a mesmerizing quality that held his attention until a soldier pushed him away from the trench with his rifle butt. The soldier gestured up the hill with his rifle barrel, and Lobeck got the message not to stand his ground. This soldier meant business.

THIS STATUE—A MODEL OF THE KECKSBURG UFO— STANDS NEAR THE TOWN'S FIREHOUSE

TAKING CHARGE AT THE SCENE

The area was soon alive with more Army trucks and armed soldiers, hushing speculations about the object as everyone wondered exactly what division of the armed forces had arrived to take charge. Western

Pennsylvania is home to many Army and Air Force veterans, but none of them on the scene that night could identify the insignia on the military jumpsuits and battle fatigues the troops were wearing. Many of them had no insignia at all. NASA personnel and men in plain dark suits wearing no badges or any form of identification joined the soldiers. Of course, none of them offered information to the curious crowd.

The Army personnel were anything but polite as they formed a cordon around the glowing object and used their guns to push the onlookers back. Members of the crowd found it odd that no local or state police on the scene were involved in the official work. Even the fire apparatus was pushed back a distance as the Army unit, now clearly starting a retrieval operation, began covering up the object with a tarp and loading it onto the huge flatbed. How did they even know they needed a flatbed that night? Had the state troopers told them to bring one along? Why were NASA personnel examining the object so intently? If this were just the crash of some kind of strange aircraft, what was NASA's business there? Whose aircraft was this, anyway?

Military police closed off all access roads and guarded the intersections, rifles at the ready, as the flatbed pulled out and headed west toward the Ohio border, presumably in route to Wright-Patterson Air Force Base outside of Dayton. It was there, almost twenty years earlier, the wreckage from a spacecraft that had crashed in Roswell, New Mexico, was brought for evaluation and testing. Now the Roswell remains would be joined by a new object of—at least as far as the public was concerned—unknown origins.

ON THE HUNT FOR ANSWERS

News manager John Murphy, who had taken the first call from one of the witnesses and who had notified the police, eventually made his way to the crash site only to find Army units blocking all access. He contacted the local state police commander for an update, but was told, firmly and finally, that there was no crash and that the police had no information. Murphy told him about police units at the scene and the presence of the Army, but was told that nothing had happened. The commander made it obvious that Murphy shouldn't ask again.

Now, Murphy was an old-time newsman and the Internet wouldn't be a household utility for a good thirty years. Like a gumshoe out of a Raymond Chandler novel, Murphy tracked down his stories by phone and in person; he showed up at people's doors with his notepad and a pencil to get his answers. This time it was no different, and Murphy smelled a cover-up. There was a story hidden in the events of the evening, and Murphy was out to break it.

He began by taking the names of some of the witnesses who had been pushed back from the crash site by the Army. Then he went back to the radio station, grabbed his little portable tape recorder, and met more witnesses at their homes to take their stories. With eyewitness reports compiled, Murphy went on the air. He boldly reported the news of the sightings, the witness reports of a crash, and the description of the object. Suddenly, Kecksburg, Pennsylvania, was the center of a fully publicized UFO incident.

THE AFTERMATH

Vince Lobeck, who had gotten so close to the UFO that he thought about touching it, began having strange pains in his joints. He kept on working, but the strain of sitting behind a steering wheel or even climbing into the cab of his truck caused him great pain in his legs and knees. He felt as though he was always running a low-grade temperature, and sores developed on the inside of his mouth. Doctors said they could find nothing wrong with him, and it wasn't until the

1990s that a doctor told him he was still suffering from the effects of an overdose of gamma radiation.

For the rest of the week after the crash, John Murphy continued to interview witnesses and broadcast reports about the UFO on the radio. But something stopped him. According to one of the receptionists at the radio station, two men who said they from the federal government showed up looking for Murphy. Through the glass window in the control room, the receptionist could see the men talking to Murphy in the broadcast booth. As they advanced toward him, evidently threatening him with something; Murphy backed away. Seemingly defiant, but still cautious at first, Murphy's posture started to sag. Finally he sat down and nodded. The men left without another word.

WHEN TO VISIT

For people wanting to go to the conference, September is the best month for traveling to Pittsburgh, Greensburg, and Kecksburg. The weather is still warm, but it is crisp at night. The damp cold that characterizes a western Pennsylvania winter, with gusts always threatening from the Great Lakes, has not yet set in.

That evening, Murphy's typical rapid-fire delivery of the news was absent from his broadcast. He spoke slowly and never mentioned the still-breaking story of the crash at Kecksburg. Instead, he said that the local state police department was reporting that despite all the rumors floating around, it was their understanding that there was no crash of any type of airplane. Even the Army denied seeing anything or being at any crash site. Murphy said the words, but it was as if a tape recorder were playing a pre-recorded message through him. According to the authorities *and* Murphy, there simply was no crash at Kecksburg.

Not long afterwards, the police found Murphy slumped over the wheel of his car on a backcountry road. They called it a "heart attack" possibly caused by drinking; the scene of his death, after all, had smelled strongly of alcohol when the police approached it. Officially, Murphy's death was listed as "natural causes." The receptionist at the station said the coroner's findings were very strange because Murphy never spoke of having a heart condition. Very strange, indeed, she said because Murphy's entire demeanor had changed after the two unidentified men confronted him in the broadcast booth. Maybe it was a coincidence, she said, but after that conversation, which she could not hear, Murphy killed the story. And without Murphy reporting the story, folks in the area just stopped talking about it. To many, it was as if the whole thing had never happened.

TODAY IN KECKSBURG

MUFON investigator Stan Gordon was just a teenager in 1965, but he has kept the investigation alive. He still writes about the Kecksburg incident, has appeared on a number of television programs—including *UFO Files* and *UFO Hunters*—and has worked with local UFO enthusiasts and witnesses to sponsor a Kecksburg conference every year. And in 2007, a group of investigators, led by former Clinton administration advisor and Obama transition chairman John Podesta, called for more open government and a release of all the files NASA might have been hiding concerning the Kecksburg incident.

For two years, NASA and the newly formed Coalition for Freedom of Information battled back-and-forth in federal court over witness statements and records NASA might have about its presence in Kecksburg in December 1965, but the search revealed no relevant documents. The question of what NASA might have been hiding remains, because if there had been nothing to hide, why were NASA personnel in Kecksburg to begin with?

ANSWERS FROM HISTORY?

THE *WUNDERWAFFE*—WONDER WEAPON

It was either a myth, a real weapon that could have changed the course of World War II, or an ongoing reality that our government has been covering up at all costs. Whatever the *Wunderwaffe* was, a former SS officer revealed its existence to the world when the Soviet NKVD questioned him after the war. The officer had worked at the Reise Mine in Poland before his capture. His colleagues had all escaped west toward the advancing American and British Armies, he told the Russians. And they took everything with them: the documents, the experiments, and the inventions. And, he said, they took *Die Glocke*, the bell, the mysterious bell-shaped object that they developed as the super weapon to win the war. If the SS officer expected his admissions and information would save his life, he was wrong. The Russians hanged him even before the United States Army Intelligence investigators could talk to him. And for some time, the story of *Die Glocke* was buried.

It wasn't until the late 1980s, as the Soviet KGB sought to raise money by selling its files that the story of this investigation leaked West again. The official Soviet report reached Polish World War II researcher Igor Witkowski through a KGB operative who had defected. Witkowski saw the notes, the drawings, and actually got a full background on the object. But as exciting and mysterious as the story may have been, no one remained alive to corroborate it. Only Wikowski's reports about the file keep the story alive.

THE ORIGINS OF *DIE GLOCKE*

The story of *Die Glocke* actually began before the outbreak of World War II when a group of five National Socialist officials led by Heinrich Himmler desperately sought information that would validate their vision of the origin of the Aryan race and establish their plan for supremacy. Their search took them all over the world: to the Middle East to search for the Ark of the Covenant, to Iceland and Greenland to search for the mysterious homeland they called "Thule," and to India to search for the Vedic texts. In India, they came upon the legends of the Vimana, the flying ships of the great Sanskrit epics. These ships, propelled by a secret liquid metal called "red mercury" had remarkable anti-gravity abilities and could transport their navigators at incredible speeds. Were these the ships of the ancient Aryans?

TURNING HISTORIC LEGEND INTO MODERN REALITY

It might have been myth, but as the members of Himmler's newly dubbed Thule Society learned, the Vedics took these stories very seriously and believed that the Vimana were real flying machines. So enthusiastic was Himmler that he convinced Hitler to give him a budget to assemble a team of engineers to research these machines. The team, led by the chief German rocket scientist and inventor of ballistic missiles, Wernher Von Braun, conducted their experiments and tests in an underground facility at a place called Mittledurer. Ultimately, according to the

> **HOW TO GET TO KECKSBURG BY AIR**
> Travelers can land at the Pittsburgh International Airport (PIT) and rent a car to Kecksburg, about forty minutes away on I-76 east.

Soviet report, Himmler's project was given such a high priority after the Russian front collapsed in 1943 that it was moved inside the Reise Mine in Poland's Owl Mountains.

An electrical engineer and SS colonel named Kurt Debus was placed in overall charge of the special weapons project. Debus was said to have engineered two counter-rotating cylinders containing a liquid metal that, when set into motion, generated a radiation field so powerful that those around it were poisoned and the object itself began to lift off vertically. The radiation was so intense that the German scientists devised a bell-shaped cockpit for the object shielded from the broad base containing the cylinders. They called it *Die Glocke*.

A POWERFUL WEAPON, BUT WITH WHAT PURPOSE?

What was the purpose of this craft? Some say that it was intended to be a supersonic anti-gravity device that could have carried a nuclear weapon to enemy capital cities. Imagine the horror of nuclear weapons detonating in the skies above Moscow, Stalingrad, London, Paris, New York, and Washington. The allies, with no defense against a war machine that appeared out of nowhere, would likely have frantically sued for peace. Even if only to buy time, a negotiated cease-fire with Germany would have left Europe under the iron fist of the Nazis and would have freed the German scientists to develop even more horrific weapons. Others, including a ninety-five-year-old Stasi officer, Dr. Axel Stol, still alive in Berlin after serving as a physicist in the East German Communist regime, have suggested an even more terrifying scenario. Stol argued, his voice still ringing with the authority of a scientist who understands the mechanism of *Die Glocke*, that it was no simple—albeit supersonic—bomber. The radiation field was so powerful that if it were able to warp time, *Die Glocke* might have been able to win the war for Germany by traveling backwards in time to alter the timeline itself. It could plant weapons to destroy the enemy even before the war began, restructuring history. Indeed, this *Wunderwaffe* could win the war even in the final minutes. But all of this might be mere speculation: no one knows for sure what the purpose of the device was.

THE FATE OF *DIE GLOCKE*

As the war wound on and Russian troops crossed the Polish border, the Germans tried to hold back the advancing Americans and

British in Belgium one last time, in hopes of buying time to deploy the *Wunderwaffe* and gain a negotiated truce that would stop the Russian Army. But when Patton's troops broke out of the Battle of the Bulge and began advancing toward the Rhine, the German high command knew the war was over.

As the snows began to melt in Poland, the Germans knew it was time to keep the object away from the Russians. Perhaps they flew their wonder weapon out on a specially designed Junkers bomber to get it to South America. Perhaps, as others suggested, the Americans discovered *Die Glocke* and flew it to the United States. Or just, perhaps, in the weeks before the Soviet army closed in on the Owl Mountains and the German's Reise Mine complex, SS Colonel Kurt Debus pushed the button—regardless of the potential casualties or the vast number of scientists and concentration camp inmates who would be irradiated—and sent *Die Glocke* hurtling into the temporal slipstream. Only he knew where it would appear.

THE INVENTOR AND HIS CREATION

Debus came to the United States at the end of the war. Along with other German rocket scientists, he was repatriated in the United States, all records of his war crimes buried deep within files at the National Archives, and was set to work recreating the missile program that reigned terror on London at the end of the war. By the early 1950s, Debus and his colleagues were hard at work on the rockets that could carry American satellites into space and potentially launch nuclear warheads against the Russians and the Chinese.

Debus, in particular, worked his way up through the NASA technical and scientific hierarchy until the early 1960s when he became the launch director at Cape Canaveral. His expertise was central to the American space programs Mercury, Gemini, and, ultimately, Apollo.

Naturally, if an object had fallen from space, Debus would have been one of the first people to know. Perhaps that's why NASA had a retrieval team in Kecksburg, Pennsylvania on the night of December 5, 1965.

Or maybe *Die Glocke* never disappeared at all. When Debus threw the switch that sent the device spinning into time, maybe it was hurtling into a very specific future. And there to meet it twenty years later as it "crash landed" just outside of a rural American town would have been none other than Debus himself.

PLENTY OF THEORIES AND SPECULATION, BUT NO ANSWERS TO SPARE

Though it is nothing more than speculation, the similarities between the design of *Die Glocke* and the Kecksburg object are so close that they seem to defy chance. Lobeck's radiation poisoning; the glowing blue-violet color; the sudden appearance of an object on radar: everything suggests that this was no simple accident. The Kecksburg incident is a mystery to this day because NASA will not release any relevant files about their eye-witnessed presence in town that night. It might well be covering up one of the greatest stories of history: the retrieval of a time machine launched by Kurt Debus into his own arms twenty years later. And all he had to do was wait for it.

▶ UFO EVENTS

Kecksburg is a charming rural village amidst the very green rolling farmland of Western Pennsylvania just forty minutes from Pittsburgh. Kecksburg has a monument to the crash of the strange object, hosts conferences every year at the firehouse, and makes witnesses available to anyone researching the mysterious event.

Every September, the Kecksburg Volunteer Fire Department hosts the annual, weekend-long Kecksburg UFO Conference and Fire Department Festival. Speakers include former fire chiefs, witnesses to the crash, and UFO researchers including Stan Gordon, who has pursued his investigation into this incident for forty-five years. Other conference weekend events include:

- The Fire Department and Rescue Squad Parade
- The Bucket Brigade contest with neighboring fire companies
- The Bed Race in which participants can customize their own beds
- Hay Bale Toss
- A concert and country music festival on Saturday
- A Native American craft market and food festival on Sunday
- A tire burning contest in which contestants hook their vehicles up to an immovable barrier and attempt to spin their tires so that the hottest tires win

And the event on Sunday night is topped off with country singers and a contest to see who can eat the hottest Buffalo chicken wings.

▶ PLACES TO STAY

There are plenty of hotels in Pittsburgh if travelers prefer staying in the city and driving out to the crash site. Accommodations are also available in smaller towns closer to Kecksburg.

The Days Inn
127 West Byers Avenue
New Stanton, Pennsylvania

Sheraton Four Points
100 Sheraton Drive
Greensburg, Pennsylvania

The Harbor Inn
805 Bethel Church Road
Latrobe, Pennsylvania

The Chestnut Golf Resort and Conference Center
132 Pine Ridge Road
Blairstown, Pennsylvania

▶ PLACES TO STAY—continued

Holiday Inn Express
250 Bessemer Road,
Mount Pleasant, Pennsylvania

The Ramada Ligonier
216 West Loyalhanna Street
Ligonier, Pennsylvania

The Youngwood Hotel
201 Depot Street
Youngwood, Pennsylvania

Mountain View Inn
1001 Village Drive
Greensburg, Pennsylvania

Comfort Inn
5064 Route 30 East
Greensburg, Pennsylvania

Bed and Breakfast Inn of Greensburg
119 Alwine Avenue
Greensburg, Pennsylvania

Econo Lodge
915 East Pittsburgh Street
Greensburg, Pennsylvania

Larry's Hotel
3401 Walnut Street
McKeesport, Pennsylvania
This is one of the closest to the
conference and festival.

▶ RESTAURANTS

Lobingier's Restaurant
114 West Main Street
Mount Pleasant, Pennsylvania

The Village Restaurant
236 West Main Street
Mount Pleasant, Pennsylvania

Smillie's Family Restaurant
6557 State Route 819 South
Mount Pleasant, Pennsylvania

King's Family Restaurant
500 Willow Crossing Road
Greensburg, Pennsylvania

DeGennaro's
1402 Broad Street
Greensburg, Pennsylvania

Cozumel Mexican Restaurant
1145 East Pittsburgh Street
Greensburg, Pennsylvania

Monday's Union Restaurant
454 Marguerite Road
Latrobe, Pennsylvania

Great Wall Chinese Restaurant
110 Unity Street
Latbrobe, Pennsylvania

Pagano's Restaurant
108 East Byers Avenue
Latrobe, Pennsylvania

CHAPTER SIX
THE HIGH BRIDGE INCIDENT

HIGH BRIDGE, NEW JERSEY

MORE THAN JUST A SIGHTING

The 1950s in America were an incredible time for flying saucers whether they were straight from science fiction movies, reported by earnest witnesses, or battled by the Air Force. It was also a decade of contact, of people like George Van Tassel and George Adamski coming forward to say that the beings visiting earth in flying saucers had a message for humans. These prophecies for the future revealed the nature of humanity's presence on earth, and the obligations that human beings have for themselves, for their progeny, and for the planet. One of the bearers of these messages of peace was Howard Menger.

PREPARING A PROPHET

Menger was born in 1922 in Brooklyn, New York, but his family moved to a farm in rural High Bridge, New Jersey when he was still young. Although his popular stories about the subject would focus on events in the 1950s, Menger's first contact with extraterrestrials actually occurred when he was only ten. In his 1956 book, *The High Bridge Incident*, Menger describes meeting and speaking with a beautiful young woman from Venus, who was sitting on a rock. The stunning, blonde-haired woman, an extraterrestrial who looked perfectly human, called to Menger using his name as if she knew him well. She told him about her home planet and the need for human beings to take better care of planet Earth. And she promised that the two of them would meet again in the future.

It would be another ten years before Menger would again see an extraterrestrial, but the memory of that first contact never faded. In 1942, Menger was in the Army stationed at Camp Cook in California when he encountered a man wearing what looked like a standard Army-issue khaki uniform. The man seemed to call Menger by name, although Menger did not know him, and spoke even though his lips didn't move. Was it a dream? Could he have really been using telepathy to communicate? The man extended his hand, and Menger took it. That instant, Menger knew that this was a palpable entity, a real life form with substance, and not just an illusion.

HOWARD MENGER

The strange man told Menger that his race arrived in North America long before the Spanish Conquistadors had crossed the Atlantic. The visitors communicated with the indigenous Aztec nation, helped them, and imparted to them special technical knowledge that advanced their civilization. The Aztecs, the man said, had become very sophisticated when the Conquistadors arrived and declared war on the Aztecs. The Aztecs never showed the Spanish conquerors the many aspects of their advanced civilization that they had received from the extraterrestrials. Because they withheld this knowledge, it died with them and never reached Europe or the rest of the Old World civilizations.

The Conquistadors were in no position to deal peacefully with the Aztecs. War and conquest had destroyed knowledge rather than preserving it. That experiment in alien-human contact had failed, but it seemed the Venusians planned to give the people of Earth another chance.

A MESSAGE THE WORLD NEEDED

In 1945, three years after his contact with the Venusian at Camp Cook, Menger received a very specific, prophetic, and overtly spiritual vision that appeared as a physical manifestation. An extraterrestrial voice told him that human beings may fear death but that there is no death. What we call death is the spirit leaving the body, but the body is just a shell, a husk. "The soul lives on," the being told Menger. The eternal entity of the soul survives, learning more and evolving as it goes through life cycles. Insofar as there is any judgment, only the good that each soul does is credited while the misdeeds are wiped away.

In many ways, what Menger reported about this conversation comports very closely with traditional Judaic tradition, which says that every time a human being does a good deed, a *mitzvah*— an angel—is created. Even one good deed—one angel appearing on the soul's behalf at the end of days—is sufficient to wipe away a lifetime of bad deeds when the time comes for judgment. Could Menger's vision be similar to many of the visions related by the Biblical prophets?

> **NOT FAR FROM HIGH BRIDGE: LAMBERTVILLE AND STOCKTON**
> Lambertville and Stockton are only thirty minutes away from High Bridge and are very convenient to the area.

The alien entity also told Menger that the destruction of millions of people was no worse than killing one person. As moving as this message would be anytime, the vision's timing made it all the more prophetic: it had come to Menger just before the nuclear bombings of Hiroshima and Nagasaki ended World War II. Both types of murder, the alien said, are wanton and bespeak evil. This is a basic evil intent, Howard was given to understand, evil in itself or *malum in se*, which denotes an evil mind. This evil intent flies in the face of what the "Infinite Father," in the contact's words, has made the law for humanity. The other type of evil, *malum prohibitum*, is the commission of an act prohibited by law and may be as simple as negligently driving through a stop sign. However the Infinite Father does not punish the evildoer. Only humankind wreaks punishment on itself and even invokes the name of the Infinite Father to impose and justify punishment on its enemies, while at the same time blaming the Infinite for its own misfortunes.

> **HOW TO GET TO HIGH BRIDGE BY AIR**
> Travelers can fly into either Newark Airport (EWR) or Philadelphia International Airport (PHL). Newark is the closer of the two at just over 45 miles east of High Bridge. Philadelphia is about 75 miles southwest.

What people don't understand, Menger said the ET told him, is that humanity is responsible for itself and for its own problems. The alien said that human beings must learn to understand how to live on this planet and recognize their civilization's place in the universe. ETs, he said, want to show us, but only if we want to learn.

His message delivered, the alien disappeared, leaving Menger alone to think about the implications of the message and their choice of him as its recipient.

A MESSAGE OF BIBLICAL PROPORTIONS

Menger was discharged from the service after the war and felt a need to return home. He was drawn back to the area in High Bridge where he wandered into the Venusian woman when he was just a child. Now as an adult, the location of his first sighting would be the setting of another.

As he walked in the woods, he saw what he thought was a floating ball of fire. But as he looked at it, he could tell that it was transforming into a flying saucer with a dome on top. The saucer actually landed, brilliant in the early summer sun, and Menger was transfixed. As he watched it settle, he saw three creatures emerge from it, all completely human in appearance. Two of the beings were men and the third was a beautiful woman—the same woman, in fact, with whom Menger had communicated fourteen years earlier in the same area.

Menger reported the conversation in his self-published book, *The High Bridge Incident*:

> **"Are you actually the girl . . . the girl on the rock?"**
>
> **"Yes I am. The same girl, Howard."**
>
> **"But you're no older."**
>
> **"Oh, but I am. Guess, Howard, how old I really am. I'm more than five hundred years old," she said. "Now you can refute anyone who says a woman tells little falsehoods about her age."**
>
> **"But you haven't changed."**
>
> **"Of course not."**

Menger couldn't believe it was possible, so she explained her people's secret of nearly ageless living. Many generations ago, she told Menger, human beings on Earth lived for many centuries. In fact, the Bible relates how the patriarchs like Abraham and Moses lived for hundreds of years. She told Howard that it was in part because the atmosphere on Earth was different and that human beings lived more in line with the teachings of the Infinite Father, the Creator. On her planet, the atmosphere is much like it was on Earth during the time of the patriarchs in Genesis—unmarred by chemicals and industrial waste; however, she reminded Menger, the lifestyle the inhabitants had on her home planet made a difference as well. She described a

THE VENUSIAN WOMAN WHO MET MENGER AT THE ROCK

kind of holistic lifestyle in which diet, mental state, and the way people socialized created the longevity that the patriarchs enjoyed in Biblical times. The world that the woman described seemed to experience an endless Golden Age of Innocence in which longevity wasn't the principal goal. The Venusians aspired to live according to the laws of the Creator, and that was its own reward.

AN EXTRAORDINARY MEETING

Menger's meetings with extraterrestrials continued, and in 1956 he sought to bring likeminded witnesses and prophets together to discuss the messages they were receiving. That August, he held an extraordinary UFO conference on the front lawn of his home in High Bridge and hosted many of his friends and neighbors—*and* extraterrestrials from the planet Venus. In fact, as UFO author Tim Beckley writes

THE CHARM OF HIGH BRIDGE

Besides having a rich UFO history and ties to extraterrestrial lore, the picturesque, rural High Bridge area is home of many attractions and a beautiful state park.

While much of New Jersey belongs to the Greater New York and Greater Philadelphia metropolitan areas, High Bridge is its own community. The town is in the rural northwestern part of Hunterdon County and is still largely farmland.

Visitors seeking conventional entertainment can relax at the High Bridge Hills Golf Club at 203 Cregar Road in High Bridge, and a regulation municipal golf course at the same location as well.

Voorhees State Park, though. may entice the UFO hunter away from the golf course. Visitors can enjoy some of the best sky watching and star gazing at the Paul Robinson Observatory of the New Jersey Astronomical Society. Contact the observatory for the park's scheduled viewing nights.

in *UFO Magazine*, Menger had become friends with author Frank Stranges and had invited him to New Jersey for the conference. Stranges is now well known for his very popular book *Stranger at the Pentagon* (1967) in which he told the story of how he had met Venusians at the Pentagon. Beckley writes that Stranges and one of his Venusian contacts, a being named Valiant Thor, was at Menger's house for the August 1956 UFO conference. Some would wonder why an alien could attend such an event without becoming the main attraction, but Stranges was able to account for Thor's quiet attendance in *Stranger at the Pentagon*:

VALIANT THOR AS DESCRIBED BY FRANK STRANGES IN *THE STRANGER AT THE PENTAGON*

> Commander Valiant Thor has the ability to appear and disappear at will. He also possesses the ability to disassemble the molecular structure of his body and reassemble himself at a distant point. This is the manner in which he vanished from the Pentagon, passing through the door of the apartment in which he was confined and carefully guarded by two Air Force Military Policeman.
>
> He then joined his brother, Vice Commander Donn, and Jill, who then appeared on the front lawn of the home of Howard Menger, in High Bridge, New Jersey. They then attended a lawn UFO lecture, where everyone there saw them. However, few of them knew or even suspected that these people were from another world.

FACING A SKEPTICAL WORLD TOGETHER

Suffice it to say that for serious UFO researchers in the 1950s and '60s, and especially today, the works of Menger and Stranges were not taken seriously. Menger, Stranges, and their Californian counterpart contactees, George Adamski and George Van Tassel, were consigned to the category of wannabe prophets. These witnesses made claims similar to Menger's: their messages came from extraterrestrial entities who were usually from Venus and who came to Earth with warnings of doom and promises of peace and harmony to those who followed their words.

Perhaps it was no accident that many of the messages from the Venusians could be correlated directly out of both testaments of the Bible. The words of the Old Testament prophets—the "promise and the curse" foretold by Moses—and the words of the disciples all offer consequences and rewards for a religious code upon which much of Western society relies. The 1950s may have ushered out a world war that saw millions of deaths and the first weapons of mass destruction unleashed on civilian populations, but the world was indeed still on edge as its most powerful nations were in possession of atomic weapons and dangerously close to an unintended nuclear war. The Venusians' messages may have been the contactees' way of confronting and condemning the deep ethical schism formed by decades of political strife.

A MIRACLE, NO MATTER WHAT YOU BELIEVE

Despite the skeptics' derision, other UFO researchers were not afraid to take a second or even a third look at Menger's claims. Tim Beckley's article on Menger cites the work of psychiatrist Dr. Berthold E. Schwarz, the prophet's longtime friend, who says he was a witness to some of the extreme strangeness surrounding Menger. In his own book, *UFO Dynamics* (1989), Schwarz recounts an incident at Menger's home when the contactee's twelve-year-old son was dying of brain cancer

As the boy slipped further and further away and after the family had given up hope in the ability of doctors to do anything for him, the

Mengers had finally turned to help from Menger's "space brothers." One witness at the Menger home that night told Schwarz how friends and family were sitting in the kitchen while the dying child was in his room with a nurse in attendance. They heard the boy suddenly cry out for his mother. Mrs. Menger ran into the boy's room, with her family and friends at her heels, to see the nurse taking his pulse. His weak heart was straining. Then the boy convulsed and a light started to shine above his head.

The witness described how the light started to glow light blue and then changed to white as it pulsated and took the shape of a bar of light. The witness said that he tried to find the source, possibly a lamp on the wall, but he couldn't find one. It was simply glowing and pulsating in the air above the boy's head. The nurse, by this time, had gone to call the doctor, but the others stayed by the child's bed as the witness saw the light grow and change shape further. Then the doctor arrived, the boy relaxed, the light was gone, and the child seemed to have recovered from the seizure and his pulse had returned to normal.

THE NEW JERSEY BALLOON FESTIVAL Nearby Readington and White House Station, New Jersey, boast the New Jersey Balloon Festival at the Solberg Airport. Every July, families can ride balloons, see an air show, and enjoy outdoor concerts, and participate in fun and games for the kids.

The witness said that he kept on looking for the strange light. He finally looked out a window and saw four men wearing "luminous uniforms" about 300 feet away from the house on a hilltop. Every one of the Mengers' guests could be accounted for, and the witness said he believed there was no way this could have been a hoax because, whom would they have been hoaxing? It was as if the Venusians had appeared to bring the child through the crisis.

Schwarz said that he believed that this was just one of many remarkable incidences in which Menger's life had been touched by anomalous events, which simply could not be explained away by conventional causality. It was as if, whether through his own efforts or through the design of something very strange, Menger was in touch with forces beyond the understanding of most people.

THE MESSENGER'S LEGACY

Though their records have preserved accounts of what could have been truly landmark events in human history, there is no extrinsic evidence to support Menger's or Stranges's claims. There are photos of the Venusians, including their commander Valiant Thor, but according to what Menger and Stranges both wrote, the Venusians' ability to transform themselves into complete human likenesses means that, even in photographs, they look no different from the rest of us. Though the images of the shape-shifting extraterrestrials are essential pieces of the High Bridge Incident, they can only be regarded as inconclusive records of a spectacular claim.

Menger's photos are certainly not the only pieces of disputed evidence in the annals of ufology, and the lack of tangible evidence to support his stories did not diminish his name and rapport among his followers and colleagues. Even now Menger is regarded as one of the true believers of extraterrestrial communication.

Menger died on February 25, 2009 at the ripe old age of eighty-seven. At his funeral in Florida, all of those in attendance celebrated his almost eighty years of contact.

▶ UFO EVENTS

After Howard Menger and his family moved to Florida, most of the activities surrounding Menger's teaching shifted with him. High Bridge itself, the town and the surrounding forests, are still visited by folks looking for the spots where the aliens appeared. Many flock to the site where the beautiful Venusian woman first manifested herself to the ten-year-old Menger, and the grounds of the Menger home where Valiant Thor and his Venusian command crew attended the UFO conference.

▶ PLACES TO STAY

Holly Thorn House Inn
143 Readington Road
White House Station, New Jersey

Holiday Inn Select Clinton
111 West Main St
Clinton, New Jersey

Courtyard Lebanon
300 Corporate Drive
Lebanon, New Jersey

The Lebanon Hotel
69 Main Street
Lebanon, New Jersey

Hampton Inn Flemington
14-B Royal Road
Flemington, New Jersey

Hampton Inn Clinton
16 Frontage Drive
Clinton, New Jersey

Comfort Inn Hackettstown
1925 Route 57 West
Hackettstown, New Jersey

▶ RESTAURANTS

Circa Restaurant
37 Main Street
High Bridge, New Jersey

Casa Maya Mexican Restaurant
1 Main Street
High Bridge, New Jersey

Burns House
4-6 Main Street
High Bridge, New Jersey

Planet Highbridge
37 Main Street
High Bridge, New Jersey

▶ **RESTAURANTS—continued**

The Fox & Hound Tavern
69 Main Street
Lebanon, New Jersey

The Clinton House
2 West Main Street
Clinton, New Jersey

The Old River House
49 Main Street
Clinton, New Jersey

The Perryville Inn
167 Perryville Road
Perryville, New Jersey

Fusion on Main
123 Main Street
Flemington, New Jersey

The Frenchtown Inn
7 Bridge Street
Frenchtown, New Jersey

The Race Street Café
2 Race Street
Frenchtown, New Jersey

CHAPTER SEVEN
UFOS OVER THE CAPITOL AND THE WHITE HOUSE LAWN

WHEN SEEING ISN'T BELIEVING

How many times has a skeptic or a debunker asked, albeit sarcastically, "if flying saucers are here why haven't they landed on the White House Lawn? Why haven't they made themselves known?" The answer is they already have. They did it in 1952, and the whole world was watching. Only the Air Force said we were only watching weather anomalies, so we did not believe our lying eyes. But even those who covered up the facts knew the truth, and they've known it for more than fifty years.

A SUMMER TO REMEMBER

The months of June and July 1952 have often been referred to as the "Summer of the Saucers," a season when UFO reports poured into the United States Air Force's Project Blue Book from all over the country. In his book titled *The Report on Unidentified Flying Objects* (1956), Captain Edward J. Ruppelt, once head of Project Blue Book, described the events leading up to the July 1952 Washington, DC UFO flap, one of the most blatant incursions of UFOs in force over restricted U.S. airspace.

In Ruppelt's build-up to his recounting of the UFOs' appearance over Washington, he writes that a swarm of flying saucers over the nation's capital was "expected." Apparently an incident at Patrick Air Force Base—the Air Force's guided missile proving ground on the Atlantic coast of Florida—during the Summer of the Saucers was the beachhead of a full-scale UFO invasion.

The incident started when a few officers were outside watching strange lights. One of the officers, believing the lights to be balloons, started a UFO joke, but it turned out that it was no joke at all. To the startled eyes of a number of officers who had gone outside to see the light spectacle, additional lights appeared. Some made hairpin turns; some stopped dead in the sky before reversing course; some changed color. And all of them defied the direction and speed of the winds aloft. They could not have been balloons.

Officers from the unit tracking weather balloons that *were* supposedly in the air that night also stepped outside to report that at least one balloon was not in the area where the other officers were looking at the light show. As the lights veered and turned, it became clear to even the most skeptical member of the group that these weren't balloons at all because a radar set was still tracking a balloon in another area of the sky. Even the normally conservative Ruppelt writes that although the lights were never identified, it became clear that any balloons in the air were already tracked by radar and identified. *These* lights were not behaving as if they were conventional aircraft or balloons and the incident had to be categorized as "unknown." But, inconclusive or not, it was all a prelude to what would occur over Washington the following night.

PRELUDE TO A FLAP

Part of Ruppelt's revelation that he *expected* a formation of UFOs to arrive in the airspace above Washington, DC included a source: apparently the captain had been forewarned by a scientist working for an agency—which he conveniently could not name—that there had been a proliferation of UFO reports all along the East Coast. The scientist predicted that because of the build-up of these sightings—and he did specifically call them "UFO sightings"—that Washington would have the "granddaddy" of all UFO flaps. And that scientist's prediction came true.

Between July 10 and July 14, the scientist's prediction started to come true. A significant number of lights started popping up in the skies above Chesapeake Bay and Langley, Virginia areas. Appearing in strange formations, there seemed to be no conventional explanation for their presence. The lights, Ruppelt said, were "too bright to be lit balloons and too slow to be airplanes." They performed maneuvers in proximity to commercial air flights from New York to Miami and just east and south of the DC area. Two men (one a scientist) standing on the ground

UFOs over the Capitol Building

at Langley on July 16 reported a formation of unidentifiable lights near Norfolk; even though there were B-26 bombers in the area, they were too far south of Langley to have accounted for the lights. This last set of lights, according to Ruppelt's investigation, were "too large to have been aircraft lights." The lights made no noise, the report went on to say, and the observers were far enough away from city noises to have heard engine noises from just about any aircraft on record. Besides, Ruppelt writes, the scientist who was observing the lights was of such national stature that if he said that these lights weren't planes then simply put, they weren't planes. And that's exactly what he said.

NOT A BIRD, OR A PLANE

With what seemed like plenty of sightings acting as an overture for the big event, the UFO flap over Washington actually began on Saturday, July 19, 1952. Radars at the DC National Airport (now Reagan Airport) picked up eight targets south of Andrews Air Force base. The targets couldn't have been conventional aircraft: according to tower radar operators on record in Ruppelt's report, the objects "loafed along" at speeds around a hundred miles an hour and then suddenly accelerated to fantastic speeds. These maneuvers were beyond the capacity of any aircraft in existence. Other planes in the area spotted the lights, visually confirming already alarming radar reports. As more reports flooded into the flight controllers around National Airport, a third tower at Andrews Air Force Base picked up an unidentified object on its scope. The situation was nothing short of urgent, and the Air Force scrambled jet fighters over Washington airspace to investigate. Now, all three towers tracked the final object together, confirming each change in position, direction, and speed simultaneously on all three scopes, and then, inexplicably, confirming when the object suddenly disappeared from all scopes at the same time. Where it went, no operator could determine, but it was gone as if it had suddenly turned itself off without giving a clue about the direction it took.

HOW TO GET TO WASHINGTON, DC BY AIR

Washington, DC, like New York and Los Angeles, is probably the easiest place to reach in the United States. After all, it is our capital, and it's served by three airports:

- Ronald Reagan Airport (DCA, formerly DC National)
- Thurgood Marshall Airport (Baltimore Washington International or BWI)
- Washington Dulles International (IAD)

But more would cement the extraordinary strangeness of that evening. A few hours later, a radar operator, saw an object on his scope and placed it right in range of Andrews Air Force Base. He called the tower personnel at Andrews to alert them. The radar operator who answered at Andrews looked in the direction where he was told and, sure enough, he saw a "huge fiery orange sphere" right where the radar said it was. This final sighting is nothing short of a full confirmation, to many, that something without a ready explanation was occurring over the nation's capital. In the world of UFO research, this kind of event—one with both visual and technical confirmation from multiple sources—is one of the most credible types of official sightings.

But as dire as the matter seemed from the ground and in the air, no one bothered to call Air Force intelligence. According to Ruppelt's report, when newspaper headlines the next day referred to Air Force jets chasing UFOs, Air Force intelligence honestly could only say they knew nothing about it. Not that the media believed them. The newspapers were even more rabid for answers, and they released headlines accusing the Air Force of being close-mouthed about the entire incident.

It wasn't until Monday, July 21, that Ruppelt—as head of Project Blue Book—was able to get any information from tower operators about what the radar picked up and what the air traffic controllers believed these objects were and were not. He found that the radar units were in perfect working order, and that the objects (whatever they were) had penetrated restricted airspace over the White House and the Capitol Building. For all the skeptics who have spent the years since the first crash at Roswell insisting that they would only be satisfied that UFOs exist when they landed at the White House, Ruppelt's findings at DC National Airport should serve as sufficient proof.

DEBUNKING THE SKEPTICS

Airports' radars are usually an easy first point of attack for skeptics, and debunkers claim that an anomaly, malfunction, or misinterpretation of the imagery is to blame for the sighting. Even Project Blue Book, the notorious debunking-and-cover-up machine, pointed to radar issues in its official report. In his book, *The Report on Unidentified Flying Objects* (1956), Ruppelt explains the radar operators at the various air traffic control tower locations in Washington, DC called in technicians the night of July 19 for the very purpose of making sure the radars were working properly. And in every case, technicians found that the radars *were* entirely functional that night. Therefore, even Blue Book's own director couldn't debunk his own reports.

Other conservative researchers have suggested that the radar operators were looking at temperature inversions or other types of false radar readings that may not have been the result of an improperly functioning radar. Inversions occur when the temperatures at higher levels of the atmosphere decrease less than normal or, in extreme cases, where the temperature at a higher altitude is actually higher than readings closer to the earth. In these cases, radar can pick up a reflection from the inversion itself. Officials quickly suggested that the DC flap was simply the result of temperature inversion, but Ruppelt argued that the radar operators were too experienced and well trained. They knew how to distinguish tangible objects from the more amorphous radar inversion anomalies, and because of their expertise, Ruppelt took them at their word.

NO REST FOR THE WARY

As much as Ruppelt wanted to stay in the DC area to continue his investigation, he could not. Military bureaucracy and red tape got in the way, and since his orders were to stay at the Pentagon for only a day, he would have been declared AWOL from Wright-Patterson Air Force Base even if he only spent a night away. Despite his own wishes, Ruppelt returned to Wright-Patterson thinking his time on the case of the Washington, DC flap was over. But he couldn't have been more wrong. He arrived in the Project Blue Book office to find that UFO sightings had been pouring in at the rate of forty or so a day. Many of these UFO reports were just as compelling as the reports coming out of Washington—if not more so. For example, in two intercept incidents off the Atlantic Coast in New Jersey and Massachusetts, F-94 jets sighted large amber lights and acquired radar locks on them. Then the lights took "violent" evasive action, the targets broke the radar locks and zoomed out of sight.

The following weekend, July 26, the radars at Washington National again reported UFOs. This time, however, the reports that crossed Ruppelt's desk didn't come from the Air Force: the Pentagon hadn't even been informed yet! Instead, *Life* magazine's resident UFO expert, who'd gotten the report from his DC bureau, called Ruppelt. Ruppelt had to set up the investigation himself by phone from his office at the Air Tactical Intelligence Command at Wright-Patterson in Dayton, Ohio.

> **HOW TO GET TO WASHINGTON, DC BY RAIL**
> Getting to Washington, DC, by rail is very easy via Amtrak, whether you're arriving from the Northeast, the South, or from the Midwest. All Amtrak and local area commuter lines use Washington's Union Station at the center of town as a hub. The station and airports are all connected by rail as well.

This time, Ruppelt asked Major Dewey Fournet to head up the investigation at DC National Airport. When Fournet arrived, Pentagon press officer Al Chop—the same man who would later take the 1952 DC UFO flap public—was already there. Now, the appearance of the UFOs would have an official audience.

CAT AND MOUSE WITH THE AIR FORCE
It was 10:30 p.m. Tower officials at DC National spotted a loose formation of slow-moving lights spread out in a wide arc around Washington—

from Herndon, Virginia, to Andrews Air Force Base in Maryland. Tower officials marked the presence of the lights on their scopes and called Andrews Air Force Base; the second tower confirmed the targets.

The separate radars tracked the targets for over an hour. The operators called for fighter jet intercepts to identify the objects and, if necessary, engage them over the restricted airspace they were surrounding. At that point, officers asked the reporters present in the tower to leave. Although the Air Force said they didn't want classified information about the intercepts leaked to the public through the press, Ruppelt speculated that wasn't the reason at all. He believed it was just in case there *were* going to be actual identifications made by the pilots. The military didn't want word of what was or wasn't in the sky to make it into the news. It was a cover-up, to be sure, though the newspaper headlines had already been spreading word about UFOs in Washington airspace for over a week.

The jets were vectored toward the location of the lights, but as soon as the F-94s arrived on the scene, the lights disappeared. The jets searched the area, but they saw no lights and returned to base. Just as the interceptors were leaving the area however, radar operators at Langley picked up targets and called the information into DC National. At that point, the DC National control tower picked up the targets over Langley and they asked a lone F-94 to try to get a visual. The pilot complied. As he pursued the target, he could see the light plainly. But in an instant it was gone, as if someone had turned off a light bulb. He reacquired a radar lock, but it was instantly broken as the object sped away. The pilot flew a search pattern over the area, locking on two more times, but every time the pilot found the object, it seemed to pick up the radar signal and broke away.

With the target over Langley gone, another formation of targets appeared on the radarscopes at DC National, Andrews, and Langley.

The towers called for fighter support again, and two more F-94s were vectored toward the target area. This time the targets stayed in the area almost as if they where waiting for the jets. But as the jets closed in and acquired their targets, the locks were broken even though the targets stayed on the scope. After what seemed like a game of

THE CHERRY BLOSSOM FESTIVAL

Whether or not there are UFO conferences in the Washington area when you visit, the nation's capital is always a great place to visit in the spring when the cherry blossom's bloom. The Cherry Blossom Festival lasts from March to April each year, when the city hosts a series of events to celebrate the world-famous trees.

The celebration commemorates both the blooming of the cherry trees along the Tidal Basin and the 1912 gift of cherry blossom trees from the Mayor of Tokyo to the city of Washington, DC.

Typically, the cherry blossoms reach their full bloom during the first week in April, a time when visitors flock to Washington to walk in amazement at the first official rite of spring in the mid-Atlantic region. But the bloom watch itself actually begins for some local residents at the end of February, when the first green buds appear on the trees. Gradually, through March, the buds grow and start to expand until, at the end of March, you can see the blossoms appear. By the next week, Washington enjoys its spring tourist season as the whole Tidal Basin area turns a bright pink.

Special festival events include:

- a night of family entertainment and a concert
- fireworks
- a parade
- a dinner cruise
- a ten-mile run
- daily theatrical events

hide-and-seek, one of the targets stayed in the area as a single F-94 pursued it. Trying to catch up, the pilot cut in his afterburner. Just as he was about to reach the target, it simply sped away, outmaneuvering and outrunning the F-94.

WHEN FICTION IS SIMPLER THAN FACT

As the first light of dawn broke on the following morning, the unidentified objects all disappeared, and the pilots began their debriefings. They explained the frustration of being unable to overtake targets that could simply speed away and disappear. When Ruppelt spoke to Major Fournet the following day, the major—who was a trained engineer—explained that the group of observers in the towers came to a consensus with which he agreed: the radar was painting solid metallic objects. These were objects, Fournet said, that could move along at a hundred miles an hour and outrun a jet; temperature inversion couldn't simply turn itself on and off in an instant or dart about an airborne battlefield. Nobody had any answers to the mystery of the unidentified targets.

By Monday morning, Ruppelt was on his way to Washington from Ohio to continue his pursuit of the truth. Despite the military's secrecy in the watchtowers, the newspaper headlines had already solved the mystery. All the major papers claimed that flying saucers had outrun the jets over the skies of the nation's capital. By the afternoon, the UFOs had become flying saucers and even President Harry Truman's Air Force liaison showed up to demand answers from the Pentagon and Ruppelt's division. During the day's long meetings, more UFO reports were flooding Blue Book's phone lines, but Ruppelt couldn't leave to investigate. He ultimately told reporters, who were bombarding him with questions, that the explanation he was working with until he could investigate further was that these were all weather-related phenomena. Ruppelt later admitted in his book that he had thrown the cover story at the newspapers just to give them something to chew on.

WHY WE DIDN'T TRUST OURSELVES

In the aftermath of this incident, occurring as it did over two weekends and involving so many verifiable sightings and confirmations, one would think that the truth would have ultimately wormed its way to the public. But, when faced with the prospect of telling the complete truth to the waiting press corps, Air Force Intelligence Director General John A. Samford agonized over what he would say. Major Donald Keyhoe—whose book *Flying Saucers from Outer Space* (1950) had become a bestseller by the Summer of Saucers—wrote that Samford was just not prepared to tell the American people that its skies had been invaded by craft that were able to penetrate right to the center of our nation's government. Convinced that the American people would panic, Keyhoe wrote, Samford indicated that the Air Force had no explanation other than weather anomalies that confused the radar and the pilots. And as wrong as his statement was, it appeared too reasonable to refute. In the coming days, even an F-94 pilot who had engaged one of the flying saucers reneged on his own story and said that he was only looking at a reflection. The tower operators, too, changed their stories and said they had only been looking at a star, but had become agitated and mistook it for a UFO.

Samford's press conference had been the key to dismantling reality into a conventional fiction. The newspapers reported the sensible statements. The press assured its readers that newsreel photos moviegoers had seen during that week of lights around the Capitol Building were simply camera anomalies, freakish weather conditions, and a star on a radarscope that caused a panic. There were no UFOs, no flying saucers, and the jets couldn't intercept anything because there was nothing to intercept.

Even though the UFOs hovered and darted over Washington during the rest of the summer of 1952, people shrugged them off. These low-flying targets still played with the jets ordered to intercept them, but the public honestly believed that they were nothing at all.

ALIEN INTELLIGENCE

The UFOs' maneuvering to break out of radar locks was just one sign that the beings piloting the crafts knew that they might have been vulnerable to our attack. And though the first nights of the Summer of Saucers played out like games, a full-fledged air-battle raged in the coming months. The UFOs weren't just passive targets: they eluded the Air Force jets whenever they could, and when they couldn't, they shot back.

FALLEN ALIENS—TAKEN DEAD OR ALIVE?
If you want to read more about the recovery of alien craft and pilots during the Summer of Saucers, check out Chapter 8!

Some American jets were targeted and blown from the sky; others simply broke apart when attempting to outmaneuver the nimble alien craft. The stories of these losses appeared in the newspapers and attributed them to test pilot crashes. But the real stories were far darker and more terrifying.

Luckily, we weren't the only victims. In fact, *Shoot Them Down!* (2007) by Frank Feschino, Jr., revealed that radar-controlled guns and rockets had indeed brought down flying saucers in the 1950s. Where they crashed and what we retrieved from them is probably a deeply classified secret and relegated to only legend and lore.

A TIME-TESTED COVER-UP

Through General Samford's debunking, the very things that skeptics had demanded of sightings and encounters had simply been explained away. But the reports of Edward Ruppelt and Donald Keyhoe, eyewitnesses to what took place over the Washington skies, debunk the debunkers. They not only detail what was really happening, but they also detail the progression of events and decisions that led to the cover-up. In so doing, they documented a critical moment in our nation's history. The year 1952, after all, was the final year of the Truman administration. Our nation was locked in a stalemate war with Korea and the government was ever fearful of what the nuclear-armed Soviets and Chinese might do if there were one mistaken calculation, one slight miscommunication. Amid the Cold War turmoil, a fleet of UFOs appeared over Washington to challenge our air defenses. The decision may have prevented panic, but in front of the very eyes of the American people, the press, and the movie camera, the Air Force told us another story so convincing we still believe it to this day.

▶ PLACES TO STAY

If you want to stay in the Beltway area, either in Maryland or Virginia, most of the major hotel chains have locations near the Metro routes. From New Carrollton, Maryland to Arlington, the Washington-area Metro system can get you to downtown attractions in under an hour. You may prefer being closer to the heart of it all, though. Here are some of the more interesting and historic hotels in downtown Washington:

Hotel Monaco
700 F Street NW
Washington, DC

The Hay-Adams
Sixteenth & H Streets NW
Washington, DC

The Harrington Hotel
436 11th Street NW
Washington, DC

The Renaissance
999 Ninth Street NW
Washington, DC

The Willard Intercontinental Hotel
1401 Pennsylvania Avenue
Washington, DC

The Washington Plaza
10 Thomas Circle NW
Washington, DC

The Mayflower Renaissance
1127 Connecticut Avenue NW
Washington, DC

▶ RESTAURANTS

From traditional Vietnamese to formal French to down-home, back-porch Southern cooking, Washington is an epicure's delight. After all, it caters to one of the largest and most demanding international communities in the world and runs on a twenty-four/seven schedule. Its restaurants have to live up to a community lifestyle more demanding than any other.

The Bombay Club
815 Connecticut Avenue NW
Washington, DC

Komi
1509 17th Street NW
Washington, DC

CityZen
1330 Maryland Avenue SW
Washington, DC

Palena
3529 Connecticut Avenue NW
Washington, DC

▶ RESTAURANTS—continued

Kotobuki
4822 MacArthur Boulevard NW
Washington, DC

Sei
444 7th Street NW
Washington, DC

Old Ebbitt Grill
675 15th Street NW
Washington, DC

Good Stuff Eatery
303 Pennsylvania Avenue SE
Washington, DC

Acadiana
901 New York Avenue NW
Washington, DC

BLT Steak
1625 I Street NW
Washington, DC

Al Tiramisu
2014 P Street NW
Washington, DC

Dino
3435 Connecticut Avenue NW
Washington, DC

Singapore Bistro
1134 19th Street NW
Washington, DC

Miss Saigon
3057 M Street NW
Washington, DC

CHAPTER EIGHT
THE FLATWOODS MONSTER

BRAXTON COUNTY, WEST VIRGINIA

FALLEN ALIENS

Mostly forgotten today, except by a small group of UFO historians is an event that has become a footnote to the 1952 Summer of the Saucers. While Air Force jets were in combat with the flying saucers, some of the jets were able to score some hits with their radar-controlled rockets. In September 1952, at least one of the saucers was shot down and came in for a crash landing in West Virginia. That same year there were other crashes, especially in the southwestern United States. Perhaps it was the ability of the Air Force to hold its own in battle, but for the second time, at least, the U.S. military got its second look at extraterrestrials, and so did some local residents.

For example, in a UFO crash in Kingman, Arizona, one story goes, the government was able to retrieve live extraterrestrials from the wreckage. Officials covertly brought them back to a secret base many believe is at one of two locations: Dugway, Utah—a weapons proving ground where we tested biological weapons of mass destruction during World War II—or the facility at Groom Lake in Nevada known as "Area 51." Other stories say that the aliens were brought to a base under construction inside the Archuleta Mesa on the Apache Nation reservation at Dulce, New Mexico, where the government began to study the extraterrestrials, allowed more to land, and entered into an unholy alliance with them to develop a joint alien/human species.

Still other stories say that representatives from the newly installed Eisenhower administration in 1953 communicated directly with what they called "the humanoid" and planned for the first human/ET exchange visits, a story fictionalized in Steven Spielberg's *Close Encounters of the Third Kind* (1977). One story says that the meetings with the humanoid were documented and notes were passed along within the closely guarded Special Access Projects protocol inside NASA, the Pentagon, and the CIA. Some astronauts may have even been briefed by CIA officials before their missions into space on the status of our government's dealings with the extraterrestrials.

But one particular story still puts people in a sleepy West Virginia town on edge some sixty years later. One of the UFOs brought down by fire from our jets in September 1952, crashed in remote Braxton County. One of the ship's weapons, a humanoid machine, began a search-and-destroy mission in the area to protect the craft until its navigators could be rescued. That humanoid creature, whether an actual life form or an android, has gone into local legend as the "Flatwoods Monster."

NOT JUST A SCARY STORY

It's easy to dismiss the Flatwoods incident as a monster story created by local residents who got spooked by a night in the woods. But that would be a mistake. The Flatwoods Monster is really a UFO story, a report of what serious investigators said was a crashed spacecraft and of the thing that climbed out of it. No less an investigator of things paranormal than the revered researcher Ivan T. Sanderson considered the Flatwoods story very significant. And within the context of the Washington, DC UFO flap, researcher and author Stanton Friedman also took it very seriously. The Flatwoods Monster was certainly a being so frightening that it etched itself into local lore in the rural backwoods of West Virginia.

Official records report that on September 12, 1952, a meteor came screeching across the sky in a bright fireball. The Air Force says that it passed over several states before plowing into a hilltop on a farm in Braxton County. That was the official explanation for the fireball. However, Frank Feschino, Jr.—the author of *The Flatwoods Monster* (2010) writes that the official records of a meteor are deliberately incorrect. The object was not a meteor and did not crash and splinter into a thousand pieces. In fact, the object made two significant turns as it slowed down in a rough S pattern. Meteors don't do that. Three witnesses—brothers Ed and Fred May and their friend Tommy Hyer— said the bright red egg-shaped object actually came to rest on top of a small rise on a farm owned by Bailey Fisher. In many ways, this part of the night was reminiscent of a scene from a motion picture released just a year later: *Invaders from Mars* (1953).

UFOs and flying saucers had been in the news for months, despite the cover story General John A. Samford had given to the press about the flying saucers over Washington, DC. So when the three boys saw the fiery object come to rest on the hilltop, they immediately ran back to the May house where they told Ed and Fred's mother Kathleen about what they'd seen. Kathleen gathered the boys and rounded up a few more witnesses for the road: West Virginia National Guardsman Eugene Lemon, two other children, Ronnie Shaver and Neil Hunley, and Lemon's dog. Together they headed back into the woods to find the crash site. As they approached the Fisher property, Lemon's dog took off ahead of them, bounding up the rise and out of sight. As the group followed the directions from the May brothers, the dog suddenly came running out of the woods as scared as any animal could be. What had the dog seen?

The group pressed on, not knowing what had spooked the dog, until they came to the top of the rise. The large glowing red object with two lights off to the side of the object was obviously no meteor. A very mysterious mist enveloped the top of the hill. The air was noxious with a pungent odor that made their eyes tear and their noses burn. It was like a heavy gas had settled over the ground, hanging low and making the witnesses feel sick. Then the two lights seemed to move and Lemon pointed his flashlight at them.

These were not lights at all, the group realized to their horror: they were eyes, the red eyes of some mysterious creature. It started hissing at them. Frank Feschino writes that the witnesses told him that the hissing sounded just like bacon frying on a skillet and that Freddie May described the noxious odor as reminiscent of an old-time radio

ARTISTIC RENDERINGS OF THE FLATWOODS MONSTER

whose tubes had burned out. On top of the scorched electric smell, it also carried the odor of rotten eggs. Through the dark and mist they could see that the creature stood ten feet tall. The monster started gliding right for them. The small band of witnesses froze, not knowing which way to run. But the creature turned and glided back in another direction, presumably back toward the glowing red egg-shaped light. At that point, the noxious mist that rose up around them like a poisonous fog began to overcome them. The witnesses felt weakened and nauseated by the fumes and by the overwhelming fear of what they had just seen. They all fled the area and ran back to the May's house.

A HUNT FOR ANSWERS

Still feeling the initial effects of the strange mist she had inhaled, Kathleen May started placing emergency phone calls to alert the public and public safety officials to what she had discovered. She called Braxton County Sheriff Robert Carr and one of the owners of the local newspaper, *The Braxton County Democrat*, Lee Stewart. Both responded. Carr and a deputy went to the area to search for evidence to support Kathleen May's incredible story. Both Carr and Stewart agreed to investigate the story together. The sheriff needed to make sure there was no immediate threat to public safety from someone running around the woods or from a craft that might catch fire, and Stewart wanted to get the story on record.

Carr searched the Bailey Fisher farm site, but he could find no evidence of an object or of the creature that Kathleen May told him she saw. For his part, Stewart interviewed a number of people and returned to the site with witness National Guardsman Eugene Lemon, where they did find traces of the noxious mist.

The next day, Stewart found the trench-like tracks at the site along the area where the May boys said they spotted the craft go down. They looked fresh and no one could account for any traffic in the remote area, but another opposing theory countered that a curious local farmer, hearing about all the ruckus in the area the night before, drove his truck to the site and made the long tracks in the dirt. But, as author Frank Feschino has pointed out, there were other signs of devastation in the area as well that couldn't be explained by the appearance of a mere farmer's truck and the tracks didn't look anything like truck tires. Some residents said they saw the monster again. Others were not so sure, but Feschino believes that what folks saw and described to him was actually a vehicle, a type of rover or hovercraft that protected the area until the ship could be repaired and flown.

ARMED WITH EVIDENCE, AIMING FOR ANSWERS

The witnesses told Feschino that the creature seemed to project an energy beam that either vaporized or burned the wood of trees in the thickly wooded area. Feschino collected evidence from the trees and found that the burn patterns were not consistent with a brush or forest fire; after all, the trees themselves were not actually destroyed.

The multiple witness testimony of the creature's appearance was also convincing because of the consistency of the stories and the descriptions. Some skeptics argue that the first group of witnesses who set out from the May house actually saw a barn owl in the woods and then panicked. These arguments raised by debunkers really don't pan out, according to Feschino, because there were too many different sightings of the creature in too many different places. Certainly, if the only people to have seen the monster were the first group of witnesses, then the story would have less credibility. But other witnesses would come across the creature in other areas, and added to trace evidence of burn marks on the trees, the consistency of the accounts lends more credence to the story.

The Air Force's official dismissal of the crash as a meteor landing also fails to explain what people saw. Feschino connects the heightened activity in the Washington, DC and Chesapeake area in the months leading up to the Flatwoods incident as actually connected to the September 12th crash landing. The Flatwoods incident, he says, did not take place in a vacuum. Attempts to describe the landing in Flatwoods as a single meteor don't work because of the number of places from which reports originated. It couldn't have been a single object because even traveling at a high speed, it would not have been able to traverse that much territory in so short a time. Moreover, different witnesses in different places described objects streaking across the sky at the same time, making it impossible for there to have been a single object.

HOW TO GET TO FLATWOODS, WEST VIRGINIA BY AIR
Fly into Charleston Airport (CRW) and by car take I-79 north to Exit 67. Private flights also land at the local Braxton County airport, which is in Sutton, a mile from Flatwoods, and is controlled by the Cleveland Center. Although a public airport, it is served by private flights.

Feschino theorizes, therefore, that within the context of all these UFO sightings, one of the several crafts seen streaking across the sky on September 12, 1952 either developed trouble and had to land or was shot down by an Air Force jet and crash-landed. And the creature that confronted the May family and their fellow witnesses? It might have been a defensive weapon to keep curious witnesses away from the craft.

Sound implausible? Think of the U.S. troops' experience in Korea and Vietnam—not to mention Bosnia and the Persian Gulf: modern militaries deploy all sorts of defensive weaponry to protect their downed fliers and aircraft, from helicopter rescue missions to heavy air cover to keep enemy troops from capturing personnel and property. Assuming for the sake of argument that this object was an alien craft, wouldn't those who brought the craft here try to deploy defensive measures as well so as to protect their crew and vehicle?

As convenient as it may be to dismiss the story of the Flatwoods Monster as a bogeyman created out of the panic of a late night encounter with a huge barn owl and a story spread by hillbillies through a backwoods county, debunking doesn't hold up well under the weight of credibility. The incident is well defended with multiple, consistent witnesses, trace evidence on the trees, and the larger context of the 1952 Washington-area flap in the Summer of the Saucers. But it *has* been nearly a lifetime since the crash; many of the witnesses have passed away and even the youngest ones are now getting very old. In the absence of any new scientific or documentary evidence, there is probably no dispositive resolution to the story.

HOME TO MORE THAN JUST ONE MONSTER

Major Donald Keyhoe made a telling commentary in 1953 when he said that of all the 1952 sightings, the Flatwoods story was "the weirdest." Not only did it consist of a real, close encounter, but it held out the greatest potential menace. Here was a case, he said, in which a witness-described "monster" was a "fearsome creature intelligent enough to build and control space ships."

The Flatwoods Monster story is, indeed, one of the more incredible stories coming out of the 1950s UFO phenomenon. It may have simply faded into local lore as "just another tale" were it not for the story of the Mothman, popularized by John Keel's novel *The Mothman Prophecies* (1975), in which strange appearances in Charleston and Point Pleasant, West Virginia, terrorized local residents fourteen to fifteen years after the appearance of the Flatwoods Monster. When you put the Flatwoods Monster and the Mothman together alongside legends like the Jersey Devil, you might ask whether human beings share this planet with a more diverse group of creatures than we realize. Some may be from here, but how many are from other worlds? Humans and such strange beings rarely cross paths, but when they do, legends grow.

▶ MONSTER EVENTS

In September of every year, the town of Flatwoods holds the one-day Monster Day Festival in the parking lot of the Flatwoods Outlet. Frank Feschino has been a celebrity guest on more than one occasion and has presented living witnesses from the town. There are portraits of the monster for sale as well as monster figurines. The Braxton County Monster Museum is also in Flatwoods and contains art, artifacts, and original stories about the appearance of the creature.

▶ PLACES TO STAY

Days Hotel
2000 Sutton Lane
Sutton, West Virginia

Microtel Gassaway Sutton
115 Reston Place
Gassaway, West Virginia

▶ RESTAURANTS

Spot Restaurant and Dairy Bar
610 Gauley Turnpike
Flatwoods, West Virginia

Ducky's Place
296 Heaters
Heaters, West Virginia

Lloyd's Restaurant
Route 4
Flatwoods, West Virginia

China Buffet
254 Skidmore Lane
Sutton, West Virginia

Sam's Hot Dog
2075 Sutton Lane
Sutton, West Virginia

Café Cimino Country Inn
616 Main Street
Sutton, West Virginia

Visions
2000 Sutton Lane
Sutton, West Virginia

La Dolce Vita
Third and Main Street
Sutton, West Virginia

CHAPTER NINE
THE GULF BREEZE SIGHTINGS

GULF BREEZE, FLORIDA

A MAN, HIS MEMORY, AND THE GOVERNMENT THAT WANTED TO STOP HIM

This is the story of Ed Walters, his UFO sightings near the Naval Air Base at Pensacola, Florida, and the extreme lengths to which some-one or some unknown agency went to discredit him. The Gulf Breeze Sightings, as they were called, stirred up a lot of controversy in 1987 when they became public. They also alerted an entire community to the possibility that they were being watched by menacing craft from another world. And like many UFO flaps, it all began with a single strange incident.

At first, people regarded Walters, a local construction manager, as just an oddball seeking publicity. But when his neighbors, local fisher-men out in the Gulf, and residents of neighboring areas made sighting reports similar to his, it became obvious that Walters had told the truth. Things became so serious, in fact, that Walt Andrus, head of the Mutual UFO Network (MUFON), personally stepped in to verify the facts of Walters's story and evaluate the photographic evidence. The Gulf Breeze sightings held the entire country in thrall through the late 1980s and early '90s.

A LATE NIGHT VISIT

Like many UFO encounter stories, the Gulf Breeze sightings began innocently enough. Walters was at home working late on the night of November 11, 1987. He happened to look up from his desk to see a light through the window that didn't look like the moon or starlight. It was brighter than a star and seemed closer than a star, but his view was partially blocked by a large tree at the edge of his front yard. Standing at the window didn't give him a better look, so he went outside to see what it was.

The intense light dazzled Walters once he was outside. He felt as if the light had noticed him as he stood there. It became brighter and larger before he realized that the light was moving toward him. As it got closer, Walters could make out that it had a definable shape. It wasn't just a blob of light; it had a shape almost like a child's top. The light descended so that it was hovering over the road in front of his house. And Walters noticed, as he looked up at it, that the object seemed to have a checkerboard pattern along its side. Were these actually windows?

As the object got closer, Walters saw a glowing, pulsating ring around the bottom. It was the strangest thing he had ever seen. He edged closer to the road to see it from a better angle and he decided that he had better get some photos, if only to prove that it was really there. So he ran inside his house to grab a Polaroid camera that was handily on his table after a long day of making construction estimates.

He quickly shot a few photos and pulled out the developed prints. Then, fascinated by the hovering object, Walters walked closer to see if he could get more detailed photos of the object's underside. The object seemed to slip directly over Walters. That's when the beam hit him.

TRAPPED!

Walters would later say that at first it was the strangest feeling he had ever had. He was paralyzed in the spot, and the more he struggled to move out of the blue beam, the more it seemed to lock him in. He became afraid, but heard something inside his mind—as if it were a

A UFO RELEASING THE SUSPECT BEAM

tape playing back a message. It calmed him, urged him not to struggle, and engulfed him in a sense of warmth as it assured him that he would not be harmed.

But how could he relax when his feet were rising off the ground? He looked down to see the ground dropping away from him even though he couldn't feel himself being lifted. He was defying gravity. Frightened, he fought as hard as he could to escape the beam, but it was no use. A hum that seemed to come from inside him filled his ears. He could smell something burning and had the taste of a sharp spice in his throat. Then, he heard a bark and could see that a neighbor was out in the street walking his dog. The beam suddenly snapped off, and Walters dropped to the ground. He ran back into the house away from the

ANOTHER GULF BREEZE UFO

object, which sped away, but the hum was still playing in his brain. The sound stayed with him through the night even as he tried to shake off the experience and get some sleep.

THE TRUTH BY DAYLIGHT AND NEWSPRINT

Even if Walters had wanted to believe that the night had never happened, he still had the photos the next morning to convince him that it had. Stunning photos captured images of a glowing, bright, articulated object that could only be described as a craft of some kind. At the very least, they proved that something strange had happened to him. He also realized that these were photographs that he had to share. Walters took the photos to the local newspaper office, the *Gulf Breeze Sentinel*, to share them with the editor and to tell his story.

Despite the shock of what had happened to him and the credibility the photographs provided, Walters was still mindful of his reputation. After all, his career as a building contractor relied on his credibility, trustworthiness, and stability. Who would hire a contractor who ran out into the street at night after a flying saucer? If Walters wanted to keep his business intact, he couldn't go crashing into the newspaper office screaming that flying saucers had arrived and were kidnapping humans. No, there had to be another way.

Then Walters figured it out: he decided to attribute the entire story to his friend, "Mr. X," who didn't what his identity to be disclosed for fear of ridicule. Mr. X had given Walters the photos and told him his story. And Walters promised to give Mr. X's story to the *Sentinel*. Seemed like a plan, and that's exactly what Walters did. But Walters's belief that his true identity would remain a secret would be quickly crushed.

NEVER ALONE

The newspaper's story about Mr. X's contact with a flying saucer caught the imagination of the community as soon as it was published. Moreover, other newspapers in the area picked up on the story as well. As the story spread, the community discovered there was more than one witness to the object on that first night. Walters's neighbors came forward to say that they, too, had seen a strange light. Before long, more and more people in the community of Gulf Breeze were reporting that something was going on in the skies above them.

Though it put his reputation in jeopardy, Walters finally revealed that he was the initial Mr. X and that he had seen UFOs again. But the subsequent sightings, which he caught on film, had turned into actual contact, and the contact was becoming increasingly menacing.

FRIEND OR FOE

Just a few days after his initial sighting, Walters heard the familiar hum in the back of his head that told him there was a UFO nearby. He also heard the sound of distant voices that he could not make out, as if they were coming from another room. Yet the hum was a constant droning in his head. Was it communicating with him? Was he simply so sensitive to its presence that he had a physiological reaction to it? Walters went outside hoping to get another photo of a flying saucer. Sure enough, he could see a light in the distance, brighter than any star and moving slowly. He was able to take a photograph as it came closer, hovered over the road, and then floated away. It was as if the object was allowing itself to be seen.

HOW TO GET TO GULF BREEZE BY AIR
Several major air carriers offer limited direct flights from major hubs around the country to Pensacola Regional Airport (PNS). You can also fly to Pensacola from one of the several international airports in Florida, including Miami International.

A few weeks later, it made contact with Walters again. This time the sighting took place sometime between 3 and 4 A.M. Walters woke from a deep sleep, alerted by the sound of his dog's frenzied barking as if there were an intruder on the property. Making no noise or commotion, Walters went to the window to see if he could see anything in the street. But when he opened the blinds to his floor-length window, he had the shock of his life.

There, separated from him by only a few inches, was the most incredible creature he had ever seen. It was the size of a child, with an oversized head, but had a completely humanoid shape. In fact, except for its proportions and very large black eyes, it could have been human. But it undulated in a strange way, as if not acclimated to our gravity or atmosphere, and did nothing else. It didn't communicate, didn't wave, didn't give any sign of recognition. Rather it only stared at Walters for a matter of seconds as he fell backwards from the shock, and then it simply moved off into the shadows of the yard.

Seized more by curiosity than anything else, Walters took off after the creature. He had to see what it was and where it was going. As soon as he stepped from underneath the roof overhang and into his backyard, that same blue beam hit him. He was instantly frozen in place while he watched the creature wander into a wooded area. Then the beam snapped off. He ran back into his house, grabbed his camera, and took off in the direction where he last saw the creature. All he could see, though, was the object hovering over the wooded area with its blue beam on. He took a photo of it and assumed that the craft was retrieving the creature he had seen.

A few days later, Walters saw the object over a nearby high school. He took his camera with him, looking for more opportunities to get proof that these weren't just delusions or hallucinations. He saw and photographed the object with its blue beam shooting down again, probably picking up the creature yet again. On another occasion, late at night, Walters saw a short, metallic, box-like creature approach the

A UFO DIPPING BELOW THE TREELINE

house from his backyard toward his dog. Walters's dog just managed to escape the creature as he hurried out to retrieve his pet. The beam only froze his leg, though, and he was able to pull himself back inside the house as the dog ran away.

Throughout the rest of 1987, Walters saw the bright craft and on a couple of occasions, he was even trapped in the blue beam. Each time, he could hear a voice inside his mind telling him, "Zehass, do not be afraid. We will not harm you." Who was Zehass? Was it a name he had been given? Were the creatures inside the craft naming him?

SUPPORT FROM EXPERTS

News of Walters's sightings caught the interest of newspapers and UFO groups across the country. Some groups, like the Center for UFO Studies, said that they thought Walters's stories were simply too fantastic to believe and that his photos looked hoaxed; other organizations, most especially the MUFON, were intrigued. Director of MUFON Walt Andrus, who had experienced a UFO sighting himself in Illinois years earlier, believed that Walters's simple Polaroid photos would have been difficult to hoax. He asked Dr. Bruce Maccabee, a U.S. Navy physicist, to analyze the photos. Maccabee concurred: the nature of the Polaroid camera would have made it difficult for an amateur to counterfeit. He agreed to analyze the photos.

Andrus also helped Walters get better photographs. He gave Walters a special four-lens camera sealed with wax so that Walters couldn't get inside to do any tampering with the film. MUFON also gave Walters a special Polaroid camera with two lenses stereoscopically arranged so that they could get a better perspective on the sizes and distances of the objects.

Maccabee remained a staunch supporter of the veracity of Walters's experiences throughout the entire research project. He even appeared on *UFO Hunters* to explain why the photos seemed authentic to him.

DOUBT AND DEBUNKING

Walters was not without his critics, even as those who would debunk his story purchased his rights for a book and a television motion picture. Tabloid newspapers offered Walters money if he could substantiate the authenticity of his photos, but though the top experts they hired couldn't completely throw out the photos, they could not absolutely vouch for their genuineness. The case simply remained open; skeptics, debunkers, and supporters all advanced strong arguments bolstering their respective positions. Meanwhile, the notoriety of the ongoing Gulf Breeze sightings spread throughout the country as people flocked to the Gulf Breeze area along Florida's Gulf Coast to see if they, too, could catch glimpses of the objects that Walters photographed.

OF INTEREST TO UFOLOGISTS
As added attractions, Pensacola is home to a large Naval Air and Submarine base, which, some ufologists say are closely watched over by UFOs. The area is also home to Eglin Air Force Base with cryogenic storage facilities that, some say, still house parts of the UFO that crashed at Roswell and the alien bodies retrieved from that crash.

TRAPPED AGAIN!

Through the remainder of 1988, Walters was under intense scrutiny. He finally agreed to take polygraph tests, which he passed on two separate occasions. He also agreed to undergo a psychological examination, which he also passed. All signs indicated that he was not lying, not delusional, and not suffering from emotional problems. The stress of the world's conflicting criticism and interest was increasing, however, and putting pressure on every aspect of his life.

As the sightings spread from Gulf Breeze to the neighboring community of Pensacola, home of a major United States Naval base,

Walters became a national celebrity. His house was also becoming something of a Mecca for UFO believers, who saw his property as ground zero for UFO contact. He appeared on a number of tabloid news shows, recounting his experiences and showing off his photos. But with the fame also came heavy attacks from the debunker community. One person said that Walters *did* have knowledge of making double exposures with a Polaroid. Some argued that he could have imposed models of UFOs onto background shots. Still others continued to offer support, saying that his photos showed no evidence of double exposure or of using wire or supports to create an illusion. Despite his book and movie deals and the accolades of those who also witnessed UFOs over Gulf Breeze, Walters wondered whether his going public with what he saw was worthwhile.

GULF BREEZE: A HIDDEN GEM
Boasting "three hundred days of sunshine a year," the northwest Florida community is one of the country's most underrated vacation spots. It is a fishing and boating community with very little of the resort energy that drives Florida's east coast and Tampa Bay areas.

Walters decided to move away from his over-popular home. The property was vacant for a period of time, but eventually its new owners moved in. According to a popular story, when the new owners arrived, they discovered a model of a UFO that looked exactly like the one that Walters had photographed. When this discovery made it into the news, the entire Gulf Breeze sighting story was condemned as Walters's elaborate hoax to gain notoriety, and six-figure publishing and movie deals. And even today, the UFO model has turned the Gulf Breeze sightings into a convenient tool to batter any and all UFO phenomena. However, Dr. Bruce Maccabee told the cast and crew of *UFO Hunters* a very different story that supported Walters's version of the facts. It also cast the Gulf Breeze sightings into an entirely different perspective, lending the flap a deeper level of veracity.

EXPERT OPINION

As Maccabee explained it, during the time that the house was vacant, an air conditioning repair and maintenance company showed up, claiming that they had been hired to inspect the pipes in the attic. They completed their work and left. After the new owners took up residence, a self-described reporter showed up at the house wanting to interview them about anything that they may have discovered since moving in. He asked if they could show him through the house to see if anything of interest might be left. The family agreed, and the group made their way to the attic. As if he knew where to look, the reporter went right to the spot near the peak of the house and miraculously discovered a UFO model. The new owners—contrary to what many newspaper reports had claimed—were completely unaware of the model's existence and were completely surprised at the discovery. The reporter in question then broke the story of the apparent hoax to the media.

If all of this sounds simply too convenient, it is. Maccabee, with good reason, asked why a hoaxer would knowingly leave behind the very piece of evidence that would prove the hoax? And in a place

Note the shadow on the bottom of the Santa Rosa Sound (1 ft deep at the shadow location). This allowed for triangulation. Calculations show
Distance: 115 (+/-)5 ft
Altitude: 38 (+/-) 2 ft
Width: 8.5 (+/-) 0.5 ft
Height: 5 (+/-) 0.5 ft

PHOTOGRAPHIC EVIDENCE THAT GIVES THIS GULF BREEZE UFO SIZE, SHAPE, AND SPEED where anyone could discover it, at that! If Walters had left the house vacant for a period of time, wouldn't he have returned to make sure he had taken all of his belongings, especially a vital prop that he had used to fake photographs? Even turned on its face, the discovery of the model simply makes no sense from an evidentiary point of view. What does make sense, however, is that someone planted the model. After all, an air conditioning company showed up—uninvited according to Walters—to perform some maintenance on an area of the house in which, some time later, a reporter without credentials easily finds a model that discredits Walters's photos. How coincidental is that?

Other people directly attacked Walters's credibility, too. A teenager and his parents claimed that the young man had helped Walters fake some of the photos. Walters's supporters argued that the parents were seeking notoriety themselves. Another critic claimed that Walters could have created the blue UFO beam in his photos by simply peeling back the print layer of the Polaroid image, thereby exposing the blue line of the coating underneath. But photo experts said that it would have been impossible to have achieved that level of precision on a single photo by peeling back the layer.

BYGONES ARE NOT BYGONES

The controversy between those who believe Walters's story and those who believe the various skeptics is still alive and kicking. Some of Walters's photographs are unexplainable, even by physicists who easily attacked other photos as being hoaxed. More importantly, many people still flock to Gulf Breeze to watch the night sky; some have even photographed objects similar to Walters's UFOs. People in Gulf Breeze still claim to see UFOs overhead from time to time, and local fishermen in the Gulf have reported unidentified submerged objects glowing in the water and following their boats. In one instance, a sailor heading back across the Gulf to Panama City spotted an unidentified submerged object rise out of the water, fly around his boat, and speed out of sight. The ongoing sightings over the past twenty-three years have kept Gulf Breeze a UFO hotspot, drawing thousands of tourists hoping for the opportunity to photograph a flying saucer.

▶ UFO EVENTS

Although it was made famous by the Ed Walters sightings over twenty years ago, there are no formal yearly UFO conferences in the area. Instead, the area is a vacation area for UFO enthusiasts seeking to visit the places where Walters took his famous photographs and where other residents in the neighboring Pensacola area also experienced sightings. Perhaps it's the easy accessibility of Gulf Breeze that draws so many UFO enthusiasts to this area year after year, especially in very early spring and in the late fall.

▶ PLACES TO STAY

The Gulf Coast Inn
843 Gulf Breeze Parkway
Gulf Breeze, Florida

Paradise Inn on Pensacola Beach
21 Via de Luna Drive
Pensacola, Florida

Days Inn
6501-A Pensacola Boulevard
Pensacola, Florida

Portofino Island Resort & Spa
10 Portofino Drive
Pensacola Beach, Florida

Holiday Inn Express
333 Fort Pickens Road
Pensacola, Florida

Hilton Pensacola Beach Gulf Front
12 Via de Luna Drive
Pensacola Beach, Florida

Comfort Inn Pensacola Beach
40 Fort Pickens Road
Pensacola, Florida

Hampton Inn Pensacola Beach
2 Via de Luna
Pensacola Beach, Florida

▶ RESTAURANTS

Peg Leg Pete's
1010 Fort Pickens Road
Pensacola Beach, Florida

Flounder's Chowder House
800 Quietwater Beach Road
Pensacola Beach, Florida

Sidelines Sports Bar
2 Via de Luna Drive
Pensacola Beach, Florida

H2O in the Hilton Pensacola Beach Gulf Front
12 Via de Luna Drive
Pensacola Beach, Florida

Native Café
45A Via de Luna Drive
Pensacola Beach, Florida

Jambalaya's
51 Gulf Breeze Parkway
Gulf Breeze, Florida

Hemingway's Island Grill
400 Quietwater Beach Road
Pensacola Beach, Florida

Tiger Point Golf Club Restaurant
1255 Country Club Road
Gulf Breeze, Florida

Billy Bob's Beach Barbecue
911 Gulf Breeze Parkway
Gulf Breeze, Florida

Crabs We Got Em
6 Casino Beach Boulevard
Gulf Breeze, Florida

CHAPTER TEN
THE STEPHENVILLE LIGHTS

STEPHENVILLE, TEXAS

FROM CHAOS TO MORE CHAOS

In late 2008 and early 2009, a strange object hovered in the sky over Stephenville, Texas. A few disconnected sightings turned into one of the most recent and exciting flaps as the object escaped when it shot off at lightning speed with a pair of F-16s from nearby Carswell Air Force Base—and eventually the Associated Press's national wires—in hot pursuit.

HUMBLE, EERIE BEGINNINGS OF A FAMOUS FLAP

The first anomaly associated with the flap was not actually a UFO sighting. It took place late in 2007, when Margie Galvez was trying to figure out what kind of animal was carrying off the chickens she was raising on her property. Night after night, more of her birds went missing until she finally decided to launch her own investigation. She installed a night vision camera in her backyard, set to start recording at around midnight. In the morning she inspected the tapes and, in almost every case, found nothing. But over Thanksgiving that year, Galvez discovered something very strange in a tape she reviewed from that camera. In the eerie gray-scale images measuring the differential between the background ambient temperature and anything generating a heat signature, Galvez saw her animals pecking the ground. Then she saw two eyes peering through the darkness. Probably a deer, she assumed. But from out of a frame at the top of her screen, a well-defined cone of white emerged. It appeared quickly as if something hovering above the ground had turned on a searchlight. The cone seemed to scan the ground beneath it, swinging back and forth like a pendulum. But, Galvez noticed, if this were a beam emitting heat, why didn't the beam appear to hit the ground? It was sharply cut off long before objects on the ground would have blocked it from continuing. The beam made three or four sweeps and then snapped up as if it were shut off. And the scene of a pastoral night returned to normal.

Galvez saved the video to a DVD and tucked it away. It was strange, to be sure, but she had no explanation for the anomaly. It would not be until the next spring, when the *UFO Hunters* came to Stephenville to investigate the ongoing flap that Galvez would show the disk for the first time and the anomaly would appear on national television.

And it would be another six months before another witness stepped forward, albeit anonymously, to reveal that she had seen what Galvez had seen. Only this witness saw it first-hand with a group of teenagers in her truck as she was driving them home from cheerleading practice. Besides the beam of light, the second witness also saw a flat, huge craft with lights and portholes along the side hovering

AN OBJECT OVER STEPHENVILLE VIDEOTAPED ON FULL-ZOOM WITH A LOW-LIGHT SHUTTER

above the railroad tracks outside of Stephenville. It was a traumatic sight that she only grudgingly revealed off camera.

A MOTHERSHIP OF A FLAP

While Galvez's video was still sitting securely on a DVD, in the evening of January 8, 2008, Steve Allen—a pilot from Selden, Texas—noticed a group of flashing white lights about 3,500 feet above his home. As reported in *UFO Magazine* by national bestselling author Jim Marrs, Allen said that the red and yellow lights formed a rectangular pattern and traveled toward Stephenville at about 5,000 miles an hour. He said that he thought the object might be as large as a mile long and a half-mile wide, much too large for any conventional aircraft. He also said that he could make out two F-16 fighters from the nearby airbase following the object after it had passed.

As a pilot, Allen was a credible witness; the details of his observations were precise and he was well qualified to analyze the direction and speed of the light pattern. Marrs, who lives in Texas and covered the story extensively, said that more than 200 other witnesses saw the lights and described them as brighter than a "welder's torch," even from the ground. Witnesses said the lights danced around each other, sometimes in pairs, and they formed patterns as they moved across the sky before disappearing. Perhaps, Marrs speculates, they only became dim so that the witnesses only saw the brightest lights. These other witnesses called the brightest light the "Mothership" because it was so large; they, too, noticed the F-16s from Allen's report.

With so many reports confirming it, that something happened in the dark that night in January is an established fact.

A SURPRISE FROM THE LOCAL MEDIA

Two days after Allen's sighting, Angelia Joiner, a staff writer for the *Stephenville Empire-Tribune* wrote her first article on the flap. Dated January 10, 2008, her article references Allen's reports as well as sightings described by Mike Odom and Lance Jones, who were out admiring the evening sunset when they saw the formations of lights. Joiner took the multiple-witness sighting seriously, and her work caught the attention of folks outside of Stephenville. As Jim Marrs wrote in *UFO Magazine*, after more than sixty years of derisive reporting on UFO sightings, local and national media suddenly treated the Stephenville sighting with a "modicum of respect." He concluded that the nature of the actual sighting itself may not have caught the nation's attention at the very first; it may have been the spectacle of local media reporting in such earnest.

Angela K. Brown of the Associated Press picked up Joiner's early articles describing sightings reported by more area residents. The early coverage on the wires was journalistically matter-of-fact: no sensationalism, no snickering at the witnesses, no side comments from debunkers or skeptics to dampen the media interest. Once the AP got hold of the story, their reporter investigated it as well. From there, the story was carried in a headline in the *Washington Post* and the Canadian Broadcasting Company.

Like the O'Hare Airport sighting in Chicago in 2006, newspapers suddenly found out that a sober UFO sighting story had legs. The U.S. national media ran with it. When Joiner and some of the early witnesses appeared on CNN's *Larry King Live*, the entire nation seemed to wake up.

THE O'HARE AIRPORT SIGHTING

At 4:30 PM on November 7, 2006, a United Airlines ground crew worker and a pilot saw a circular object in the sky before it shot up through the cloud cover and disappeared. They alerted control tower personnel who could not verify the sight. United Airlines investigated per FAA regulations, generating a series of e-mails in which its personnel described the object. But the airline and control tower publicly denied that any incident occurred. Transportation reporter Jon Hilkevitch of the *Chicago Tribune* secured copies of the e-mails and FAA audio tapes and wrote an article asking why the FAA and airline would deny a safety incident when the witness descriptions were a matter of public record. The article generated over a million hits on the newspaper's website.

MORE INFORMATION ALWAYS BRINGS SKEPTICS

As in the O'Hare case, readers became so interested in the UFO story, that they hit the newspaper websites again and again, ringing up the page visits as they constantly sought updates on the story. And from Texas, the updates kept making the news. Steve Allen's assertion that he saw F-16s chasing the formation of lights, for example, prompted AP reporter Brown to seek proof. She contacted the 301st Fighter Wing at the Joint Reserve Base Naval Air Station at nearby Fort Worth to find out if they had any F-16s in the air that night. Fighter Wing spokesman Major Karl Lewis said, in a statement reported in the *Stephenville Empire-Tribune*, "no F-16s or other aircraft from this base were in the area the night of January 8, 2008, when most people reported the light sightings."

Major Lewis said he believed that people saw two commercial air-liners whose paths were crossing. To folks on the ground, he said, it might seem as though the two sets of navigation and running lights would look like one set of lights on a huge craft. The fact that the lights were moving in one direction also might indicate that a large craft was moving across the sky. But people in Stephenville quickly dismissed that suggestion. First, the lights were observed over the course of many nights, not just on one occurrence. And, second, different people in different locations saw the same exact set of lights which seemed to be moving with respect to each other, not simply right and in formation. It was only Steve Allen who said he was able to perceive a rigid structure to the light formation even though all the witnesses agreed that the lights seemed to be able to move in pairs.

> **HOW TO GET TO STEPHENVILLE BY AIR**
> Stephenville is about a ninety-minute drive from the Dallas Fort-Worth International Airport (DFW), which is serviced by all major airlines flying out of all major metropolitan-area airports.

"IF IT'S NOT OURS WE'RE IN TROUBLE . . ."

One of the most dramatic sightings was reported by local resident Rick Sorrells in an interview with UFO investigator and author Linda Moulton Howe. Sorrells said that though his sighting was not only stunning in itself, the aftermath and official attempts to silence him told him what he saw was inconveniently real.

On his way out to hunt, Sorrells realized he was standing about 300 feet underneath a massive object above his tree canopy. Through the scope of his rifle, he saw only a "mirage"-like haze coming off of the object, as if it were emitting the kind of heat that makes a highway blur in the sunlight.

Jim Marrs quoted Sorrells's description of his experience extensively in his article on the Stephenville lights in *UFO Magazine*:

> I really didn't know what to think. I was not scared, so I dropped my gun. And then I really started noticing how big this thing was. I also noticed that it had these round indentations. They were in a grid pattern all running left to right and front to back. They were all placed about forty feet apart. They were deep, like maybe four to six feet deep into this craft.
>
> It basically looked like a piece of sheet iron that had been pressed. I couldn't see any nuts; no bolts, no rivets, no welds, no seams. I was really studying the structure of this trying to get an idea about how it was built. It is huge!
>
> I've actually been back into the woods and looked. In my mind, I did the football field measurement. I know it was longer than three football fields. ...While I was looking at this [craft], it drifted to the right by about one hundred feet. And I remember looking to my left to see if I could see the edge of this thing. And I could not see the edge of it. I turned back to my right, and I was like, Wow, this is crazy!

And now, I'm rushed with emotion as far as What is it? What is it going to do next? Do I need to get out of here? I still haven't formed a conclusion. I really don't know. I hope it's our military. I hope we have something that is this advanced.

If it's not ours, then we're in trouble. I don't know the capabilities of this thing to move at such speed that it has and as big as it is. Does it have the capability of weapons? I don't know. But if they can build this, I'd sure hate to see if they got mad at us! You know what I'm saying?

Sorrells claimed that he had been harassed by various agencies as a result of his decision to go public. One evening, he was threatened by a person in uniform who told him to keep quiet about his sightings. It would be for his own good, Sorrells said the person told him, because no one would believe him anyway and that he was just making himself sound kooky. But Sorrells had become a media favorite, instead, setting the stage for more favorable reactions to witnesses' accounts in the future.

COUNTEROFFENSIVES BY THE SKEPTICS

What had Sorrells seen? One explanation advanced by a number of science experts was that the early evening sightings people had were only "sundogs," the reflection of the sun on ice crystals in the sky. But this doesn't explain either the light sightings or Allen's and Sorrell's sighting of a rigid object.

Some people dismissed the lights as a training exercise out of Fort Worth in which jet fighters were dropping either ground illumination flares or phosphorescent chaff. This counter measure generates a heat signature so intense that it lures heat-seeking missiles away from the jet. These same explanations had been offered a decade earlier to account for the dramatic Phoenix lights that captured the world's media in 1997. But the flare explanation never accounted for the strict formation and movement of the lights. And still another military explanation argued that folks saw a jet guarding President George W. Bush's ranch at Crawford. That, too, would have made sense if Crawford weren't seventy-five miles away and if President Bush had been at the ranch that night.

> **MORE THAN A PIT-STOP!**
> If you're on a UFO road trip on your way from the southeast across the bottom of the country to Roswell, New Mexico, Stephenville is well worth a weekend or longer. You can stop in to the local bookstore for local history about the town's relationship with UFOs and spend time in one of the most historic locations in Texas.

AN HISTORIC RETRACTION

While the explanations and counter-explanations flew back and forth, the 301st Fighter Wing added another twist: they announced that their original press release saying that there were no jets in the Stephenville area on the night of January 8, 2008, was in error. In fact, they said, they had made a mistake because there were actually *ten* F-16s in the air that night on a training mission. This time—for the first time in a long time—the news media was skeptical of the official Air Force statement. Reporters said that the Air Force realized they needed an explanation and suddenly reversed themselves to save face. As area residents also said that much nighttime activity for ten planes would have involved so much personnel and so much money that they doubted the Air Force could have pulled it off without lots of ancillary activity around the training exercise. People called the Air Force story a hoax—but one that still supported witnesses' claims. The lights seen on January 8 were not conventional aircraft.

UFOLOGISTS ON SCENE

With newspapers buzzing around the state and commentators on the local news carrying interviews with Stephenville lights witnesses, the Mutual UFO Network decided to catalog witness interviews to establish a careful record of the sightings. State MUFON Chairman Ken Cherry and Texas Chief Investigator and Assistant State Chairman Steve Hudgeons brought eight additional investigators to Stephenville to interview as many witness as chose to come forward. As Jim Marrs and Angelia Joiner reported, Cherry said that the number of sightings in the Stephenville area was well beyond the normal few sightings a month for that area of Texas and numbered well over a hundred. That told him, after he had eliminated the conventional possibilities, that witnesses were probably seeing similar things in the sky and that the sighting reports formed a pattern. It was time to collect all of the sighting reports and correlate the common elements.

On January 18, Cherry, Hudgeons, and their MUFON team assembled the witnesses in Dublin, Texas, a small town south of Stephenville. The overwhelming presence of the media startled the outsiders. The phenomena of seventy-five members of the media present to cover the interviews overshadowed the strong rally of witnesses

THE COWBOY CAPITAL

Stephenville and surrounding Erath County calls itself the Cowboy Capital of the United States with good reason. Erath County has had some of the richest prime grazing land in Texas. Also, the great cattle drive trails headed north from Abilene crossed through the Stephenville area, which became the home to all sorts of saddle and blacksmith establishments to service the cattle drovers. Today, visitors to Stephenville can find dude ranches and cowboy entertainment in the area.

who showed up. More than that: 600 people—who were not witnesses themselves—flooded into Dublin to hear the reports. The small town had one of the worst traffic jams in its history. At the meeting, Cherry and Hudgeons collected 200 witness reports, both in writing and verbally, and secured videos and photographs as well.

GATHERING THE FACTS

What made the media and the public take these sightings so seriously? Cherry believed that the nature of the witnesses themselves, even more than the nature of the sightings, caused the media and the public at large to sit up and take notice. This was "middle-class America coming forward," Cherry said. "Not just some jokesters coming out of the woodwork." The witnesses, he told the newspapers, were actually pillars of their respective communities. They were pilots, flight attendants, peace officers, farmers, ranchers, and generally very sober people who are not given to flights of fancies or to hyperbole.

Together, MUFON investigators, the UFO Hunters, and Angelia Joiner of the *Empire-Tribune* worked to evaluate the sightings. In one case early in the sightings, town constable Lee Roy Gaiton saw a large triangular object hovering over the road outside of town and captured it on video. The UFO Hunters also interviewed a state public safety officer who was in the patrol car alongside Constable Gaiton that night; the second witness said that they could make out a rigid shape to the object, much like witness Steve Allen did, and to their eyes looked nothing like the conventional aircraft that the 301st Fighter Wing said were in the air that night.

> **DON'T ROCK THE BOAT!**
> Over the course of sixty years of UFO investigations, witnesses were generally regarded as kooks or malcontents. The media ridicule was often so intense that many credible sighting reports never made it into the public arena, for witnesses' fear of being cast as unreliable.

MUSIC FOR YOUR EARS AND FEET!

Fans of Country and Western music will enjoy many of the clubs that are located in Stephenville. There's Texas two-step dancing, old-timey country music, lots of guitar pickin', and some of the liveliest banjo strumming and fiddling west of the Mississippi. One local favorite: The Cross Timbers Opry on Highway 377.

Other residents volunteered to return to the places where they saw the object for an experiment. With a balloon lit and tethered to a line so that it would head in the same direction that witnesses reported, different people in different locations were able to pinpoint both the object's position and its direction. The experiment showed that it would have indeed been possible for witnesses in different locations around town to have seen the same object on the same night.

Some witnesses provided some intriguing video of objects they said were part of the Stephenville flap, but many of the videos were from handheld minicams and could not stand up to a pixel-based analysis because of lens distortion, under- or over-focused video, and discoloration of the image resulting from extreme close up shooting while in night vision mode.

MORE DATA TO ANALYZE

It's always possible that these UFOs weren't extraterrestrial at all. One conjecture by military analysts and reporters was that these objects were top-secret observation platforms that were capable of neutral buoyancy or even anti-gravity. Platforms such as these could scan an area with infrared—which is what showed up on Margie Galvez's video—or electron beams to scrub for any electronic data or heat signatures. The government, in these instances, would rather folks believe them to be extraterrestrial craft than military weapons because it helps keep the technology secret. As one CIA agent was reported to have said, "It's a good thing for UFOs because if they didn't exist we would have to invent them."

In July 2008, Texas MUFON research director Robert Powell worked with radar expert Glen Schultze to investigate the radar tapes from various air traffic control locations and revealed two things. First, based on the witness reports correlated with radar tapes on the nights in question, Schultze and Powell determined that there *were* radar targets in the sky and that these targets were the sightings that the witnesses reported. (In other words, these sightings were not mere delusions or fanciful wishful thinking; they were real.)

The other interesting discovery from the radar report was that the object or objects witnesses saw were indeed heading toward President Bush's Crawford Ranch, in its time known as the Western White House. The information lends itself to a lot of speculation about what type of object would be heading over to the Crawford Ranch, but given the size of the object and the indications that this was not a plane—there were no transponder returns that the radar tapes reported—one can only wonder what it was. An Air Force or intelligence agency top-secret aircraft flying stealth might not return a friend or foe transponder reading. But one would think that *any* type of aircraft flying near as restricted a zone as a presidential residence would have to identify itself or be intercepted. Might that have been the reason that the object was chased by two F-16s? In the absence of any documentation, one can only speculate.

The Stephenville lights are seen off and on to this day, but now they're being taken almost in stride by Stephenville residents who know they do exist, even if they don't know whose they are.

> **NOT THEIR FIRST TIME IN TOWN**
>
> As reported in local newspapers a hundred years earlier and by town historian Sarah Canady, who helped research the town's UFO history for *UFO Magazine*, Stephenville has had a long history of UFO-related events. One of the first UFOs spotted in the West landed in the center of town back in 1897, though it was just a metal-clad balloon on its way to Cuba to fight the Spanish on the eve of the Spanish-American War!

▶ UFO EVENTS

The Texas MUFON chapters hold monthly meetings in the Dallas/Fort Worth areas as well as in Austin, Texas. According to Steve Hudgeons, one of the primary MUFON investigators of the Stephenville lights, the Stephenville story is always on the agenda, and guests are always welcome.

▶ PLACES TO STAY

You don't have to go all the way to Dallas or Fort Worth to find a nice place to stay.

Best Western Cross Timbers
1625 W South Loop
Stephenville, Texas

Days Inn Stephenville
701 South Loop
Stephenville, Texas

The Econo Lodge
2925 West Washington
Stephenville, Texas

La Quinta Inn and Suites Stephenville
105 Christy Plaza
Stephenville, Texas

Hampton Inn Stephenville
910 South Harbin Drive
Stephenville, Texas

Holiday Inn Express
121 Lockhart Street
Stephenville, Texas

▶ RESTAURANTS

There are plenty of quiet home-cooking restaurants in Stephenville for folks who don't want to make the hour drive to the Fort Worth Stockyards. Also, because Stephenville is a college town, the home of Tarleton State University, there are plenty of nearby taverns and grills catering to the college crowd.

Hard Eight BBQ
1091 Glen Rose Road
Stephenville, Texas

Montana Restaurant
1376 West Washington Street
Stephenville, Texas

Jake & Dorothy's Café
406 East Washington Street
Stephenville, Texas

La Fiesta Mexican Foods, Inc.
1044 West Washington Street
Stephenville, Texas

▶ **RESTAURANTS—continued**

Jalisco Restaurant
865 West Washington Street
Stephenville, Texas

Golden China
Bosque Road
Stephenville, Texas

Grumps
1645 West South Loop
Stephenville, Texas

Fiddle Creek Steakhouse
2004 Swan Street
Stephenville, Texas

Lonesome Dove Western Bistro
2406 North Main Street
Fort Worth, Texas

Riscky's Barbecue and Burger
140 East Exchange Avenue
Fort Worth, Texas

CHAPTER ELEVEN
AREA 51

RACHEL, NEVADA

COMMON—BUT ESSENTIAL—KNOWLEDGE

Question: Where is the best place in the United States to see a UFO?
Answer: the desert in Rachel, Nevada, outside of the top-secret Air Force Base known as Area 51. The facility has been top secret since the 1950s, but many suspect Area 51 is where extensive reverse engineering of exotic craft took place. It is the home of the infamous SR-71 Blackbird, and, quite possibly, the home of experimental flying saucers developed from craft that had been shot down or had simply crashed. If hundreds of witnesses over the past thirty years can be believed, Area 51 is a required stop for anyone interested in an introduction to flying saucers.

DON'T TRY IT AT HOME

Of course visitors can't get onto the actual base itself. There are posted signs around the base threatening any intruders with lethal force. Microphones that ring the base pick up the conversations of anyone planning a quick run onto the property. Sensors along the road can pick up the sound and vibrations of any vehicles coming too close, and video surveillance cameras provide the security teams on the base a full situational awareness of goings on around the perimeter.

For people who get too close, they can see what investigators have called the "camo dudes" get into their Humvees, turn their lights on, and move slowly toward the base perimeter. People who trespass are subject to arrest by the Lincoln County sheriff, if they're lucky not to have crossed the base's security perimeter. If they do make it across, they are subject to the use of lethal force by the guards. In some cases, intruders who have made it onto the base before being stopped have been subject to follow-up questioning by various federal agencies including the FBI and the Defense Intelligence Agency. The government takes the security at Area 51 very seriously.

CHOICE VIEWING

The best place to see UFOs is the Nevada desert outside the base. A long, slow drive along the perimeter in the middle of the night—the optimum time for UFO sightings—during the period that the Air Force is testing its secret weapons might just reveal a huge flying triangle hovering over your car. Many people have seen it. Alternatively,

AUTHOR AT THE INFAMOUS WARNING SIGN OUTSIDE AREA 51

if you're camping out in the desolate wilderness around the base in an RV equipped with computers, scanners, and digital cameras, you might see strange lights zipping back and forth across the sky.

Seemingly caring very little who might be tracking them, these lights perform hairpin turns at high speeds, vertical climbs and descents, and what can only be described as a cloaking device rendering them invisible in place. Are they ours or theirs or both? Visitors to Area 51 can make their own decisions if they're lucky enough to see a huge craft floating over the desert and accompanied by fighter jets.

THE BIRTH OF A LEGEND

The mystery surrounding Area 51 began during President Dwight Eisenhower's administration when the Air Force expressed its need for a new base. They wanted it to be in the middle of nowhere with enough space for extra long runways to accommodate the large spy planes that were then under development. Also, the base had to be secure enough that workers there could be sequestered for periods of time to focus on the engineering and design and, importantly, the reverse engineering of other craft to develop new generations of advanced aircraft.

THE ROAD ON WHICH SO MANY HAVE SIGHTED—AND PHOTOGRAPHED—UFOs

Because military operations in the United States take place within areas known as Military Operations Areas, or MOAS, testing for advanced aircraft have to take place within especially large MOAS so that all aspects of a flight test can be evaluated. The Nevada desert fit all the requirements and Lockheed's Skunk Works selected the base in 1955 for development of the U-2 spy plane and eventually the SR-71 Blackbird and the Stealth fighters and bombers. More specifically, Groom Lake—a salt flat nestled inside a particularly large MOA—was perfect. It is even close to the historic testing area at Edwards Air Force Base in California.

The rumors of Area 51's existence began in the 1970s. It was said that technology from the UFO crash at Roswell—a crash that the Air Force and the United States government have steadfastly denied ever happened—found its way to the secret Nevada facility for the purposes of research and reverse engineering. Despite numerous attempts to get confirmation from the Air Force regarding the existence of the base, the Air Force has refused to comment upon either the actual existence of an Area 51 or what might be going on at the base, should the base actually be acknowledged.

The mystery around Area 51, and its connection to secret UFO technology became public in November 1989, when Bob Lazar—a self-described former Area 51 employee—appeared on KLAS television with news correspondent George Knapp to talk about the reverse engineering of alien technology at the base. In an exclusive interview,

UNDER LOCK AND KEY

The secrecy at Area 51 is so tight, even for employees, that there is no public transportation system to get people onto the base. Employees don't simply show up at the front gate and present an ID card for admittance. Not at all. To get onto the base, one has to be either flown in or driven in on secure flights or buses. Former employees have said that they commute back and forth to Area 51 out of McCarran Airport in Las Vegas on a special airline called "Janet Airlines." When UFO Hunters tracked the Janet Airlines planes, they found that the tail registration numbers indicated the passenger aircraft belonged to the federal government. Janet Airlines, others have said, is a carrier owned by the Central Intelligence Agency. Employees have also described buses with blacked-out windows that transport them to and from the base as well.

Lazar revealed to Knapp that he had been employed at Area 51 as a specialist to help reverse engineer the propulsion systems of alien craft so that they could be developed for military use. But Lazar's story, as wild as it sounded over twenty years ago, was not without substantiation.

Lazar contacted Knapp to break the story of what was going on outside of Las Vegas. He was a man in trouble, he said, because he had violated his secret clearance to save his marriage. Lazar's wife didn't believe that he was really going to work at a secret base. To prove it, he took her and a friend out to the base because he knew the nights the "alien reproduction craft" would be flying over the base's airspace. When his bosses at Area 51 realized he had broken security, Lazar's clearance was pulled and all of his employment records and past history were erased. This was the story he presented to Knapp and the world.

To corroborate his tale, Lazar took Knapp and former CIA pilot John Lear out to the desert to see some of these flights for themselves. Lazar demonstrated that he knew when the test flights would take place and knew the location where his guests could see them. And

HOW TO GET TO AREA 51 AND RACHEL, NEVADA

Unless you have special clearance into the base, you'll be driving through Las Vegas. To drive to Area 51—and from there to Rachel—from Las Vegas, take I-15 northeast out of Las Vegas to exit 64 where it intersects with U.S. 93, also called Highway or Route 93, where you head north, through Alamo, to Highway 375. Take 375 to Groom Lake Road, make a left, and you're on your way to the entrance to Area 51. You will first pass Groom Lake.

Continue along the same road and you will begin to see high scrub along the highway. This scrub brush conceals video cameras and microphones. You can head up to the main gate. To get to Rachel, take Groom Lake Road back to 375 and turn left. Go straight and you will get to Rachel and the Little A'Le'Inn.

Lear, one of the most decorated test pilots in the history of the United States, was convinced of Area 51's existence at Groom Lake. He has since stood up to vouch for Lazar's story even in the face of aggressive debunking and skepticism.

Lazar explained that even though he first believed that he was only looking at very advanced, top-secret *terrestrial* technology, when he saw the interior of the craft he speculated that it had been reverse engineered from a technology alien to us. Lazar also told Lear that he had seen various documents that gave him the impression that Area 51 was housing alien technology. Lazar said, and Lear has explained it in scores of television interviews since, that he believed the fuel essential to advanced space travel was an element he called "Element 115."

The craft, as Lear has explained it, doesn't move through space. The propulsion system is so intense that it actually draws space to and around the craft, almost like a slipstream effect, so that the craft stays in one place while space and time pass around it. Lazar said that he once saw a demonstration in which he was told to look through the glass pane of a door into a room where a candle was flickering. Someone turned on a beam of focused Element 115 and the candle stopped flickering. Although Lazar couldn't account for that phenomenon, he was told that the beam actually stopped time around the still burning candle. This was how the craft was able to traverse huge light-year distances across space.

> **HOW TO GET TO LAS VEGAS BY AIR**
> All major airlines service McCarran International Airport (LAS), which is only minutes from downtown Las Vegas and the Las Vegas strip.

EVIDENCE OF TRUTH OR TROUBLE?

As one can imagine, the Lazar story and his appearances on KLAS television stirred up a huge controversy in 1990 and alerted the folks at

THE EXTRATERRESTRIAL HIGHWAY

This stretch of road running through the infinitesimally small town of Rachel, Nevada, is the main tourist attraction. Driving in the dead of night through the Nevada desert near Area 51 or along the ET Highway is an experience well worth the travel because it is entirely possible that folks may see a very strange craft. Stories about flying triangles hovering over cars along the highway or lights in the sky zipping back and forth abound.

Area 51 that the ufologists were on to them. As more and more UFO sightseers traveled to the desert to try to get onto the base or take pictures of the base, the government became more and more concerned about security.

Meanwhile, researchers who tried to find out more about Lazar discovered that he was simply a "nowhere man," a guy with no past or identity. Lazar claimed that the government erased it, but his critics said that there was no record of his working at Area 51 or at any other high-tech institution because he was simply a hoaxer or delusional. Knapp, however, managed to discover references to Lazar in administrative literature at Area 51, thus establishing to his satisfaction that Lazar was telling the truth and that he was a worker at the base.

Just recently, a number of former employees at Area 51 have gone public with their stories of working at the base. They talked about working on the nation's first spy planes and reverse engineering Soviet aircraft in what they called the A-12 project. These are top-secret operations because the United States obviously didn't want to allow the Soviets any inside intelligence regarding our surveillance capabilities. At the same time, none of the former employees who went public stated they ever saw any UFO technology. As far as they were concerned, it didn't exist.

The former employees' testimony notwithstanding, one engineer from the base named T.D. Barnes revealed that although he never saw any extraterrestrial technology, it would have been possible for a group to work on a development project without anyone else knowing about it. Barnes said that the work force at Area 51 was so compartmentalized that no one knew what anyone else was doing. Moreover, people at the base were forbidden to discuss their respective work with anyone else—even other Area 51 employees. Therefore, if a group in the next building were working on a flying saucer, they should have been the only ones who knew about it.

Countless tourists visit Area 51 just to see if they can snap a photo of a UFO. The area is isolated, desolate, and so well protected that even approaching the base, someone will trigger surveillance camera hidden in the scrub brush alongside the road and microphones buried just beneath the surface of the sand. The guards and military personnel at the base know you're coming and are well prepared for it. But because the site has become

A FAVORITE REST-STOP FOR UFO HUNTERS IN NEVADA

a Mecca for ufologists, people will walk up to the "no trespass" signs just to get their photos taken there. The guards do appreciate that and leave casual visitors alone.

▶ PLACES TO STAY

If you're traveling to Area 51, whether you're flying to Nevada or driving from Los Angeles or points east, you will drive in to the city of Las Vegas where there is no shortage of hotels and motels. Las Vegas has a hotel and casino for every taste, predilection, and wallet. Of course, *the* place to stay in Rachel is the world famous road stop, restaurant, gift shop, museum, hotel, and RV park combination: The Little A'Le'Inn at 1 Old Mill Road. Its unique character and relationship to the area is an experience in itself. However, book reservations there well in advance because it is a tourist draw and there is no guarantee that rooms will be available. They even have an RV park! Take a look at these other local hotels and RV parks:

Alamo Inn
367 N U.S. Hwy 93
Alamo, Nevada

Windmill Ridge
2111 Old Windmill Spur
Alamo, Nevada

Alamo Auto Motel
Highway 93
Alamo, Nevada

Alamo Truck Stop
Highway 93
Alamo, Nevada

"R" Place RV Park
Highway 93
Hiko, Nevada

▶ RESTAURANTS

If you're staying in Las Vegas, you have a choice of three or four restaurants, bars, clubs, and even coffee shops in every single casino on the Las Vegas strip. In downtown Las Vegas, there are also many restaurants to choose from ranging from gourmet establishments to very modest coffee shops. Rachel and Alamo also have plenty of places to grab a bite closer to the base.

The Little A'Le'Inn
1 Old Mill Rd
Rachel, Nevada

The Shack Pizza
151 Broadway
Alamo, Nevada

Alamo Truck Stop
Route 93
Alamo, Nevada

Windmill Ridge
2111 Old Windmill Spur
Alamo, Nevada

CHAPTER TWELVE
THE HICKSON/PARKER ABDUCTIONS

ON THE DOCK OF THE PASCAGOULA RIVER

On October 11, 1973, in the small town of Pascagoula, Mississippi, shipyard workers Charles Hickson and Calvin Parker were fishing off a local pier on the Pascagoula River when a large dome-shaped craft suddenly appeared. What started out in the media as almost a joke—two guys talking about being picked up by a space ship and seeing the aliens inside—turned into one of the most important UFO cases in the 1970s. The case was investigated by Dr. J. Allen Hynek, the consultant to the USAF's Project Blue Book who developed the "close encounter" designation and its categories. Hynek said the Pascagoula abductions case was more than "interesting:" it smacked of something "not terrestrial." This was quite an endorsement of the story's veracity by the nation's top skeptic, who later turned believer. But there are always layers of a sighting to investigate, and no matter how credentialed the supporters, any encounter needs extrinsic evidence to support it.

FROM LIGHTS ABOVE A CITY TO TERROR ON A PIER

The incident actually began the day before in St. Tammany Parish near New Orleans when two police officers saw a strange flying object apparently gliding over a housing project. The next night, the incident continued when forty-two-year-old Hickson and nineteen-year-old Parker sat fishing on a pier on the Pascagoula River more than 100 miles away. Whatever they were talking about, a strange whirring sound completely alien to the normal sounds of the river caught their attention. The sound was like an electrical motor turning. They looked up from the water to see two blue lights coming toward them. To their

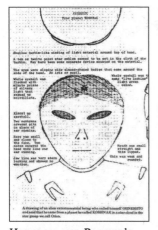

HICKSON AND PARKER'S SKETCH OF THE CREATURES THEY SAW COMING OUT OF THE CRAFT

horror, they noticed that the blue lights were part of a cigar-shaped object floating in the air. The object had a dome shape on top of it. It kept coming toward them.

The thirty-five-foot-long craft floated up to the two shipyard workers and hovered about two feet above the water. It was motionless. As Hickson and Parker stared in disbelief, a door opened on the craft and three strange-looking creatures emerged. These were no human beings. They looked more like reptilian life forms and wore no clothing. They stood on legs that seemed fused together and were able to walk with stiff movements as if they were metallic or mechanical men.

The creatures, about four-and-a-half to five feet tall, had rough, scaly, skin, no apparent eyes or mouth, and no neck. Worse, Hickson and Parker remembered, the creatures had crab- or lobster-like claws instead of hands. This description, of course, made their stories seem unbelievable to the public, but they stuck to them.

Hickson and Parker were paralyzed immediately by a beam that emanated from the craft, and could only watch as the claw-creatures approached them. They were powerless to resist, their arms frozen at their sides. The pale creatures with rough skin, as scaly as the skin of a reptile, levitated Hickson and Parker off the ground, grabbed them, and floated them through the air into the ship. Parker said that he was so frightened at this unearthly experience, he passed out completely. The description of what happened inside the ship and the scanning procedures that took place all came from Hickson, who remained conscious but paralyzed, throughout the entire series of events.

Hickson said that he was floated a few feet from the deck inside the craft and got a better look at the creatures while something that resembled a huge lens or even an elliptical-shaped eye seemed to scan his body. Hickson said that the creatures themselves had no eyes, at least not eyes that he was able to make out. And instead of mouths, the creatures had tiny slits. They did not speak to him at any time during the encounter but seemed to communicate with each other by making "buzzing sounds."

MAKE A VACATION OF IT!
If you are planning to visit Pascagoula, consider combining it with trips to New Orleans and Gulf Breeze. The drive between these cities is very picturesque, and there are plenty of things to see along the Gulf Coast.

The scanning of both men lasted less than a half an hour after which time, Hickson and Parker were floated out of the ship by the creatures and guided back to the same dock from where they had been originally abducted. By this time, Parker had regained consciousness; Hickson believed he had not lost track of any time. Both men were fully cognizant of what had happened and accepted the fact that it was real and not a joint hallucination or a dream. Accordingly, both men were absolutely terrified about what they had seen and what they experienced. They walked back to their car and just sat there for almost an hour as they tried to accept the magnitude of their encounter with something disturbing and unearthly.

At first Hickson and Parker tried to confirm with each other what they already believed had happened, but their minds needed time to accept the terrifying encounter. They started discussing what they witnessed from the beginning: the whirring and buzzing sound, the lights and the craft, and being seen and taken by the creatures. It was time to confront what to do next.

TELLING THEIR STORY . . . OR TRYING TO

At first they thought that no one would believe their incredible story. Unearthly creatures, a hovering flying saucer, being probed and scanned and floated back to the dock: none of it seemed believable even though they knew it actually happened. They decided that they should report it to the Air Force because they had heard about the Project Blue Book investigations. They made the call to Keesler Air Force Base in nearby Biloxi, Mississippi, hoping to get in contact with someone there who would take their report and push it up to the office that handled UFO encounters. But an official answering the phone told them that they had to go to the local police. The Air Force, the official told them, no longer handled UFO reports because its official investigation had closed down five years earlier.

> **HOW TO GET TO PASCAGOULA BY CAR**
> U.S. Highway 90 runs right through the center of the city. Since U.S.-90 intersects with Interstate 10, the transcontinental highway, all major north/ south interstates connect with an easy route to this UFO hot spot.

In essence, as far as the public was concerned, what Hickson and Parker were told was entirely true. The Air Force had closed down Blue Book years earlier. However, the Air Force still investigated—and still investigates to this day—serious UFO sightings that might just be real and constitute a threat to any restricted airspace in the United States and U.S. bases around the world.

But as far as Hickson and Parker were concerned, the Air Force had no interest. Thus stymied in their initial attempt to report their encounter, Hickson and Parker ultimately decided to follow the suggestion from the Keesler personnel and go to the police.

At 10:30 that night, Hickson and Parker walked into the Jackson County sheriff station, where they told their story to the desk sergeant and ultimately to Sheriff Fred Diamond himself. The sheriff could see that both Hickson and Parker were agitated and clearly traumatized by something. Yet they had no proof, no evidence to support their story of having been abducted by strange creatures. The only thing they could substantiate about their story was that the fact that they were fishing because they brought a fish they'd caught into the station. Of otherworldly creatures and strange craft, Hickson and Parker had no proof whatsoever.

Diamond had nothing to go on. Hickson had admitted he was drinking after the incident, which cast doubt on his veracity. But the sheriff had an idea. If the men were hoaxing up a story, they might trip themselves up if they were put in a room under the belief that they were all alone and might continue to concoct their plan. The sheriff would eavesdrop on their private conversation and tape them. If they were concocting a hoax and revealed that in their conversations, then when confronted with the tape as evidence, they might confess and the whole matter would be closed. But that's not what happened at all.

> **HOW TO GET TO THE PASCAGOULA AREA BY AIR**
> The Pascagoula area is serviced by two airports: Mobile Regional Airport (MOB) in Alabama, and Gulfport-Biloxi International Airport (GPT) in Mississippi. Both airports are serviced by multiple airlines from every major urban airport in the United States.

A PRIVATE CONVERSATION EXPOSED

The two men, left alone in a room with a concealed microphone, immediately began to talk about the incident as if it were real. They remained in a state of shock. Parker said he wanted to see a doctor to get some sleeping pills because he was so nervous, that he was "damn near crazy." Hickson kept remarking about Parker's physical state when "they" carried him out of that "goddamned thing." Parker complained that his arms had simply "froze up" as if he had stepped on a rattlesnake and had been paralyzed by the venom.

Parker also remarked that he had never passed out before in his entire life. That experience alone was that terrifying. For his part, Hickson kept remarking about how he had never seen anything like what had happened to them before. But the problem would be making people believe a story that was out of this world. Hickson warned that people had "better wake up," though. He figured that what happened to them would happen to others. In any event, the creatures' presence alone was enough to cause alarm. And both men seemed astonished at how the door of the strange craft seemed "to come right up." It was fantastic and terrifying. Then the two men got even more nervous being alone in the room and said they wanted to go home. Hickson still hadn't told his wife, Blanche, about the incident.

PICTURE PERFECT
Pascagoula is one of Mississippi's largest cities, its fishing village blending with ante-bellum mansions with huge oak trees covered by Spanish moss.

FACING PUBLICITY AND SCRUTINY

Despite the taped conversation, the sheriff was still skeptical that this incident actually took place. The men seemed genuinely panicked about it and talked about it as if it were real, but the sheriff still had no *evidence* to go on. Hickson and Parker said that they would take lie detector tests to show the sheriff that they were telling the truth.

Back at work on the following day, Hickson and Parker told parts of their story to coworkers, but when the sheriff called to tell them his office was flooded with reporters wanting to know the details of their otherworldly encounter, they were shocked. They had wanted to avoid any exposure at first because they rightly believed that the public at large would think they were a couple of kooks or worse: they could have been cast as publicity seekers who made up a fantastic story just to get public notice, sell a book, or get a deal for one of those television movies that were just coming out. No, they wanted to be out of the public view at first and just recover from what they described as a traumatic experience. But that was not to be.

The sheriff said that reporters from all over were badgering him for answers to this encounter story and he wanted them to come down to the station to get the reporters off his back. Hickson's foreman at the shipyard overheard Hickson's story and took it to the shipyard boss who, in turn, suggested that Hickson and Parker engage an attorney to represent them. The attorney set up a meeting with officers from Keesler Air Force Base, who interviewed them along with Air Force intelligence officers.

In the end, Hickson passed a lie detector test set up by the attorney. Though the polygraph test should have been conclusive, it was conducted by an inexperienced polygraph operator. Arch-debunker Phil Klass later poked holes in the results because of the operator's lack of experience, although the test still showed that Hickson believed

> **LA POINTE KREBS HOUSE**
> Built in 1718, this building was taken over by the Spanish, then later by the British. It is the oldest structure in the Mississippi Valley, built out of seashells held together by mud used as a mortar. Its eighteen-inch thick walls were built to withstand musket fire.

the story he was telling. Both Hickson and Parker left Pascagoula because of the overwhelming publicity surrounding the event. Parker finally suffered from a nervous breakdown due, Hickson said, to Parker's difficulty in accepting the terrifying event that they both endured.

FROM DEBUNKING FACTS TO SUPPORTING WITNESSES

In an article in *Rolling Stone Magazine*, writer Joe Eszterhas said that during his investigation of the event, he found that toll booth operators who had a full view of the area where Hickson and Parker were fishing could see nothing during the time period the men claimed to have been abducted. The security cameras at the nearby shipyard showed nothing unusual. However, a few days later after the event, a truck driver traveling just east of the Pascagoula River claimed that his vehicle was beamed up into a strange craft and that he was examined by small creatures. In 2001, Naval Chief Petty Officer Mike Cataldo came forward to say that he and crewmates were driving along Route 90 from Pascagoula on the night of the Hickson/Parker incident and saw a saucer-like craft traveling over the highway. It had flashing lights and a flat shape like a "tambourine." At first Cataldo thought it was just a group of flashing lights before he realized it had a definite shape. The UFO seemed to be hovering over a clump of trees after it crossed the road, and then took off. Cataldo was not the only person to have seen the object: cars on the road slow down to look at it. Back at his base the next day, Cataldo reported what he saw to his superior officers, but none of them did anything about it. Finally, he called a public information officer at Keesler Air Force Base, but he didn't believe the officer ever did anything about his report. He only found out about Hickson and Parker's sighting after he was on temporary duty in California. Ultimately, Cataldo's report made it into the Pascagoula case file.

A SUCCESSFUL ENDING
Charles Hickson also told his story on the Dick Cavett show and ultimately wrote and self-published a book called *UFO Contact at Pascagoula* (1983) about his and Calvin Parker's experience.

▶ PLACES TO STAY

The La Font Inn
2703 Denny Avenue, U.S. Hwy 90
Pascagoula, Mississippi

Villager Lodge Pascagoula
6007 Highway 90
Pascagoula, Mississippi

Studio 6
4419 Denny Avenue, U.S. Highway 90
Pascagoula, Mississippi

Super 8 Motel
4919 Denny Avenue, U.S. Highway 90
Pascagoula, Mississippi

▶ RESTAURANTS

La Fiesta Brava Mexican Restaurant
3223 Denny Avenue
Pascagoula, Mississippi

Aunt Nita's Seafood and Burger
4935 Denny Avenue
Pascagoula, Mississippi

Scranton's Restaurants
623 Delmas Avenue
Pascagoula, Mississippi

Catalina Seafood
1925 Denny Avenue
Pascagoula, Mississippi

Bozo's
2012 Ingalls Avenue
Pascagoula, Mississippi

Hong Kong Palace
1312 Telephone Road
Pascagoula, Mississippi

China Garden
3141 Denny Avenue
Pascagoula, Mississippi

La Font Inn
2703 Denny Avenue
Pascagoula, Mississippi

Kevin's Korner
1611 Market Street
Pascagoula, Mississippi

Monica's Kitchen
3109 Pascagoula Street
Pascagoula, Mississippi

McElroy's On the Bayou
705 Bienville Boulevard
Ocean Springs, Mississippi

CHAPTER THIRTEEN
THE KOKOMO LIGHTS

A SIGHTING THE COUNTRY TOOK SERIOUSLY

The story made the National Terror Alert website. It was covered by local and national newspapers. And it was featured on a number of television news shows. At the heart of the uproar was a large explosion and fireball hovering over a very quaint midwestern town that defied a conventional explanation regardless of all of the skeptics, who said it was only a flare dropped by an F-16. How many times does a possible encounter between two UFOs reach the level of a national terrorism alert? Answer: when the encounter is frightening enough to require a nonthreatening explanation.

AN EXPLOSIVE EVENT

The incident took place on April 16, 2008 in Kokomo, Indiana—a town with a landscape right out of a Currier & Ives print. Many of the town's residents were literally thrown out of their beds that night by a huge concussive bang that shook the entire county area. Those who were able to compose themselves ran outside into the night to see a dazzling orange circle hanging in the sky. Others saw the same globe, but it was at first ascending and then descending. Alongside it, witnesses saw a string of lights come on, one after the other. And then the orange ball and the string of lights disappeared.

Like many UFO incidents, this one began with residents who were either tucking themselves into bed at 10:30 P.M. or sitting down to work in their home offices. The sudden, loud boom and shock wave rattled windows and felt like an earthquake. The shock wave was so intense that it was felt not only in Kokomo, but throughout Howard County and in neighboring Tipton County.

But Kokomo, Indiana isn't the place you'd expect UFO stories to blossom. Sixty miles north of Indianapolis, it is a small, closely knit, bedroom community. The folks there are not given to wild flights of fancy, do not routinely see lights in the sky they can't explain, and are used to seeing F-16s off in the distance in the nearby Military Operations Area during exercises by the Indiana Air National Guard. When the shock wave and boom hit, literally knocking some people out of their chairs, folks considered it a serious and credible event. They immediately called 911 to alert emergency services. The switchboards were overwhelmed within minutes with operators reporting later that boards were so backed up they couldn't even get to the calls.

Frightened people ran out into the streets to see what caused the boom, and what they saw startled them even more. The huge orange ball of light looked almost like a mid-air explosion, hanging low over the horizon. And within minutes, as the

ORBS ABOVE KOKOMO

shock wave rippled across neighboring communities, other residents reported seeing a string of lights over the horizon where the orange ball of light had been. Some of the residents were U.S. Air Force veterans and even they said this was nothing like any aerial phenomenon they had ever seen before. One witness, who lived near Grissom Air Force Base, said that she had seen F-16 exercises in that area before on many occasions and knew that this ball of light was neither a flare nor an F-16. She had never seen its like before. After the explosion, she said that she saw F-16s in the air, even though the base later reported that its planes were all on the ground fifteen minutes before the boom. But if it didn't look like a plane, what did it look like?

Many of the witnesses and first responders to the loud boom and lights over Kokomo said that they actually saw a light spectacle that night instead of simply a large exploding ball in the heavens. A former sheriff's detective and an Air Force Vietnam War veteran, who said that he had handled flares in the service, said that he was close enough to the phenomenon to see more than the huge orange ball of light and the string of lights that followed. He said that after the lights in a string were all on, they began turning off, one after the other, in the exact order that they had come on. It was as if, he said, the lights were attached to a circular object that rotated, bringing each light into view before rotating them away again. Could these lights have been attached to a saucer-shaped object that came into view as the object rotated?

> **HOW TO GET TO KOKOMO, INDIANA BY AIR**
> Kokomo is about an hour's drive north on Route 31 from Indianapolis International Airport (IND), which is serviced by most major airlines.

The former detective and Air Force serviceman said that he stared at the light spectacle for as long as it was in the air. It played out almost as if there were two separate craft he was seeing. One craft seemed to have exploded into the orange ball. The other craft spun next to it and displayed the string of lights. Almost beyond speculation, the witness said that one could surmise that one craft was helping the other—or the two craft had been involved in some sort of battle. One witness who called 911 reported that he'd actually seen an aircraft disintegrating in the air. It seemed to explode and flaming fragments flew in all directions. But the mystery was only beginning to unfold.

MANY POSSIBILITIES, FEW ANSWERS

The first and most obvious explanation was that an aircraft might have already flown away but left a string of flares and that's what the residents saw. However, conversations that MUFON investigators had with residents revealed that many of them had witnessed flare drops in the area because Grissom Air Force Base and the Air National Guard at Fort Wayne were close by, and flare exercises were sometimes a nighttime recreation for many folks. They said they often gathered to see ground illumination flares dropping in the nearby Military Operation Area.

The lights witnessed on April 16 didn't look like the flares residents had seen in the past, they told investigators. For one thing, most flares hang in the air for a relatively short period of time. These lights were visible to some people for over an hour, way too long for flares. Moreover, the F-16s out of Fort Wayne were not allowed to descend below 30,000 feet and were not allowed to break the sound barrier in the Military Operations Area. Thus, low-hanging flares and a low-flying plane breaking the sound barrier would have been a violation of the flight rules.

Some skeptics advanced the suggestion that the explosion might have been an airplane that later crashed. Calls to 911 even *reported* what sounded like a plane crash. Police and sheriff's units fanned out across the two-county area around Kokomo to look for the crash site. However, by the time units arrived at what they believed to be the scene, there was no debris. This immediately led to reports that something—perhaps a flying saucer—had crashed and special recovery and retrieval teams had already cleaned up the area. However this, too, seemed unlikely: it was dark and the police arrived so quickly that even if the recovery teams were on site immediately, it would have taken too long to remove every scrap of debris. And no sign of wreckage was found at any of the suspected crash sites.

Still, if someone wanted to stage a cover-up it would have been possible. Speculation about a UFO crash was fueled by 911 instructions to police and fire units in the field to switch to an "incident-one" frequency, thereby taking the communications off the main dispatch channel. If an order had gone out to cover up the activities of police and rescue teams that night, the hushed communications would have eliminated the chances that anyone with a police or fire radio scanner could listen and record the transmissions. But the lack of any debris field or the absence of any military or even black trucks or SUVs in the field still made a UFO crash cover-up unlikely.

Yet another explanation that was advanced was that a meteorite had crashed. While that wouldn't explain the string of lights that people said they observed seeming to hover in the air, it might explain the orange fireball. Even though the fireball didn't seem to move along a trajectory as if it were an object falling through the atmosphere, in the panic of the moment, witnesses might have been mistaken about what they saw. The investigation just didn't turn up enough evidence to support this potentially debunking theory.

In the weeks following the incident, searchers looked for anything that might have been a meteorite impact crater in what they believed to be the crash area. But the only hole they found was probably a sinkhole; the ground had collapsed sharply and in order to dig a hole that vertically, the meteor would have had to have come straight down. Most meteor impact craters are angled and show evidence that the fragment from space actually plowed along the surface before imbedding itself in the dirt. Also, if a meteor did impact the earth, it would likely have exploded fragments over the area, some of which would have dug their own craterlets.

Some UFO debunkers also argued that the lights people saw hovering in the air might have been earthquake lights, which arch or spark from the build-up of electric potential when certain substances are subject to extreme stress—particularly the grinding of plates beneath the surface of the earth in an earthquake. Earthquake lights are the result of piezoelectricity, the creation of an electric field from certain ceramic materials under stress. The debunkers pointed to earthquake activity north of Fort Wayne, miles away from where the lights appeared over Kokomo, as evidence of the possibility that an

THINGS TO DO AROUND KOKOMO

If you're planning a trip to Kokomo with family, there are plenty of other attractions to see besides the night sky. What most people don't know, for example, is that Kokomo was the birthplace of the automobile. Kokomo is the town where inventor Elwood Haynes built the first horseless carriage in 1894. Haynes also invented stainless steel and metal alloys that are still in use today in the U.S. space program. The area has many cultural attractions related to Haynes, the car, and the nation's history.

The Elwood Haynes Museum
1915 South Webster
Kokomo, Indiana

The Grissom Air Museum
1000 West Hoosier Blvd
Grissom Air Force Base, Peru, Indiana

The Kokomo Automotive Museum
1500 North Reed Road (US 31)
Kokomo, Indiana

The Kokomo Opalescent Glass Factory
1310 South Market Street
Kokomo, Indiana

The Greentown Glass Museum
112 North Meridian Street
Greentown, Indiana

The Seiberling Mansion
1200 West Sycamore
Kokomo, Indiana

earthquake could have been responsible for the lights witnesses saw. But a professor of geology at Indiana University quickly put the damper on that theory by explaining that there has to be a serious earthquake to generate a significant electric field for lights to appear. No such earthquake took place in the Kokomo area.

In the days after the initial boom and after the Air National Guard said that they had no planes in the air on April 16, 2008 after 10:15 P.M., they released a subsequent statement saying that there was one F-16 in the air after all that had returned to base. The ANG said that the craft released a missile avoidance flare—chaff—low to the ground and then, as it sped away, it broke the sound barrier by accident. The pilot was chastised for generating a sonic boom against regulations. The Air National Guard said that this explained what the witnesses heard and saw, and they apologized to the residents of Kokomo for the anxiety that this incident created.

THEY SAW WHAT THEY SAW

This should have shut down any further speculation about the cause of the boom and dismissed any UFO theories once and for all. But the local residents denied that the lights they saw were flares; they'd all seen these training maneuvers before and were sure they hadn't seen these types of lights in the past. The line connecting the lights was too straight, some said. Others who described the line as hovering instead of falling pointed out that all flares descend. And the Air Force veteran and retired homicide detective said that if an F-16 were dropping flares that close to the ground and then breaking the sound barrier, witnesses would have heard the roar of jet engines over the shockwave and sound of the boom.

He also said that a typical sonic boom is really two claps of sound: one from the pressure created by the nose of the aircraft, and the other created by the tail assembly of the aircraft. The closer the plane is to the ground, the smaller the distance that the pressure waves have to travel and the closer together the two sound claps occur. For the sound he heard to have been a single boom, he explained, the aircraft would have had to have been below 1,000 feet, perhaps even closer to 500 feet above the ground. Not only would this have broken all the flight exercise regulations for operating so close to a residential area, the sound of jet engines would have been so loud that they would have been heard over a twenty-mile radius. Absent the sound of jet engines, he said, he had to dismiss the theory that a lone F-16 caused the boom.

ONGOING INVESTIGATION

There has been no satisfactory explanation of the 2008 lights. Witnesses and residents are still concerned about even more recent reports of Kokomo area light sightings. Multiple witnesses have reported orange balls of light in the sky—OBOLs, witnesses have called them—either accompanied by or followed by strings of lights in a perfect straight line. Most of these spectacles occur at around the same time every night: 10:30 P.M., ostensibly after Grissom Air Force Base is closed and with no reported activity from the Air National Guard in Fort Wayne.

If these are UFOs, what could they possibly be looking for in northern Indiana? Residents don't know, but the state director of the Mutual UFO Network in Indiana says that in addition to the large balls of light, residents continue to see smaller floating orbs at night as well.

The Kokomo area continues to be a UFO hotspot. For folks wishing to see unexplained balls of light in the sky and see floating orbs first hand, even possibly interacting with them, Kokomo might just be the place for an interesting summer vacation.

▶ PLACES TO STAY

Bavarian Inn Bed & Breakfast
4697 Dixon Road
Kokomo, Indiana

The Belfry Bed & Breakfast
311 West Walnut Street
Kokomo, Indiana

The Lazy AA B&B Guest Ranch
10799 West 100 South
Russiaville, Indiana

The Comfort Inn
522 Essex Drive (US 31)
Kokomo, Indiana

Courtyard Kokomo
411 Kentucky Drive
Kokomo, Indiana

Days Inn & Suites
264 S. 00 E.W. (US 31 South)
Kokomo, Indiana

Fairfield Inn Kokomo
1717 East Lincoln Road
Kokomo, Indiana

Hampton Inn & Suites Kokomo
2920 South Reed Road
Kokomo, Indiana

Holiday Inn Express
511 Albany Drive
Kokomo, Indiana

The Kokomotel
4112 N. - 00 E.W.
Kokomo, Indiana

Motel 6
2808 S. U.S. 31
Kokomo, Indiana

Jameson Inn
4021 South LaFountain Street
Kokomo, Indiana

Super 8 Motel
5110 Clinton Drive
Kokomo, Indiana

Quality Inn & Suites
1709 East Lincoln Road
Kokomo, Indiana

And for families traveling in RVs, there is the Spring Hill Campground at 623 S. 750 W. in Kokomo.

▶ RESTAURANTS

In addition to all of the restaurant facilities at the local hotels and bed and breakfast establishments, visitors will find some great food at:

17th Street Café
1135 South 17th Street
Kokomo, Indiana

Artie's Tenderloin
922 South Main Street
Kokomo, Indiana

The Book Nook Bistro
311 West Walnut Street
Kokomo, Indiana

The Breakfast House
3111 South LaFountain Street
Kokomo, Indiana

Ms. Mary's Southern Cooking
1245 South 17th Street
Kokomo, Indiana

Grindstone Charley's
3830 South LaFountain Street
Kokomo, Indiana

The Half Moon Restaurant & Brewery
4051 South LaFountain Street
Kokomo, Indiana

Olde Oak Door
2130 West Sycamore Street
Kokomo, Indiana

Whiskey Creek Wood Fire Grill
490 South Reed Road (US 31)
Kokomo, Indiana

The Quarry
2130 West Sycamore Street
Kokomo, Indiana

Dynasty China Buffet
3734 South Reed Road (US 31)
Kokomo, Indiana

Kyoto Japanese Steak House
311 East Lincoln Road
Kokomo, Indiana

Enriques Fine Mexican Food
1714 West Boulevard
Kokomo, Indiana

Country Catfish Restaurant
268 South Reed Road (US 31)
Kokomo, Indiana

Buffalo Wild Wings Grill & Bar
1803 East Markland Avenue
Kokomo, Indiana

CHAPTER FOURTEEN
THE ROSWELL INCIDENT

THE HEARTLAND OF AMERICAN UFO HUNTING

Roswell, New Mexico, isn't just a vacation stop or even a must-see. A trip to Roswell is a pilgrimage to the beating-heart central of UFO history in America, the mother of all UFO incidents, and the paradigm changer that began it all. From the earliest moments after base commander Colonel "Butch" Blanchard ordered his public information officer Lieutenant Walter Haut to tell the press that the United States Army Air Force had retrieved a crashed flying saucer from the desert outside of the city of Roswell, the Army set in motion an ongoing drama about what it recovered and why officials kept changing the story. What can we say really happened at Roswell in July 1947? What is the military hiding?

AMERICA'S FAVORITE CRASH STORY

Most people know the basic story of what happened at Roswell. In July 1947, one or two strange-looking craft crashed in the desert outside of town. The crash and debris field were reported to Chaves County sheriff George Wilcox by rancher Mac Brazel, who gave Wilcox some of the debris to store in his jail. Wilcox called Blanchard, the base commander of the Roswell 509th Army Air Field, who dispatched his intel-

ligence officer Major Jesse Marcel to
the site. Marcel returned to the base
with some debris, stopping at home
to show it to his son, Jesse, Jr., who
is still talking about that night today,
over sixty years later. The next day, the
Army released the news that it had
retrieved a flying saucer from the desert. And on the following day, Marcel was ordered to bring the debris
to Fort Worth, where 8th Air Force
commanding general Roger Ramey,
ordered a red-faced Marcel to kneel
down in front of a weather balloon
and admit that he'd made a mistake in
identification. And that was how the

**MAJOR JESSE MARCEL EXPLAINING HIS
"ERROR" TO THE PRESS CORPS**

story ended until 1978, when Marcel went public with the news that
he *had* retrieved a flying saucer and that he could not keep silent about
what really happened.

NOT A CLOSED CASE

The real story of Roswell has been told in any number of books, motion
picture documentaries and dramas, and in many television episodes,
including *UFO Hunters*. Given the basic, reported elements of the
Roswell incident it may seem like nothing new can be added to this
tale. But no matter how many times the story is revisited, there always
seems to be some new fact that was overlooked in the past. And to
keep the excitement bubbling, there are still living witnesses—some
too frightened to reveal what they remember—who can talk about
the live ETs pulled out of the wreckage, the nature of the debris they

retrieved, and the threats Army Counter Intelligence Corps (CIC) personnel made against them.

In their book *Witness to Roswell* (2007), researchers Tom Carey and Don Schmitt interviewed Roswell residents who knew the original witnesses. They offered details from reports by people actually at the base when the Army brought the alien pilots back from the desert.

HOW TO GET TO ROSWELL BY CAR

By car, most folks get to Roswell by taking either west I-40 through Albuquerque and heading east to Roswell or north Interstate 25 through Albuquerque and driving south. Either route will take between three and a half and four hours.

Their subjects included the engineer from Boeing Aircraft who inspected the wreckage to determine what kind of propulsion system the craft had used; Jesse Marcel, Jr. who actually handled the alien material that his father brought back from the crash site; Sergeant Earl Fulford, now deceased, who was part of the debris retrieval team; and retired Lieutenant Walter Haut, who revealed not only what he actually saw at the crash site and back at the Roswell Army Airfield, but the methodology of the cover-up as devised on orders from higher-ups in Washington. These witness revelations are not just hearsay. They are actual eyewitness accounts that would be admissible in any court. They describe the specifics of what happened in early July 1947.

THE STORY, RETOLD AND WITH NEW SOURCES

For example, sheriff George Wilcox's wife Inez—who kept a private diary of her work at the Chaves County jail in Roswell—wrote that Wilcox called the Roswell Army Airfield to report the debris Mac Brazel had brought in from Foster Ranch. And that was how the Army got involved.

According to author Tom Carey, a collision between two spacecraft caused the crash that spread debris over the ranch. Either they were battling each other or had experienced faulty navigational controls, but the collision sent them in different directions. The one saucer-shaped craft skidded along the ground, ejected a crash pod containing its pilots, and came to rest at the side of an arroyo. The alien pilots—possibly extraterrestrials, possibly time travelers, possibly beings from another dimension—were thrown from the craft. At least one survived, one was critically injured, and another was killed. All three were brought back to the Roswell Army Airfield along with the debris from the crash site.

Witnesses at the base, including a maintenance worker, actually saw the creatures and years later described them to their children. One of the fire fighters who was dispatched to one of the multiple crash sites also saw the creatures, watched the Army recover the debris, and brought back to the firehouse a piece of a strange metallic substance that bounced back into shape when it was crushed. His daughter actually played with the strange piece of metal and remembers it today as if it were still in her hand. Sergeant Earl Fulford also remembered handling the strange metallic foil—he called it "memory metal"—at the crash site because he commented

> **HOW TO GET TO ROSWELL BY PLANE**
> Most major airlines serve Albuquerque International Airport (ABQ), where you can rent a car for the shorter drive east on I-40.

that he could not easily stuff the material into his gunnysack when he and members of his team were ordered to collect all the debris.

The director of the funeral home in Roswell, Glenn Dennis, described being asked by the Army to assemble small coffins for children. And a nurse at the hospital also recalled seeing the aliens, being told not to talk about what she had seen, and being disciplined for disclosing what she saw. Wilcox, too, and many other witnesses were all ordered to keep quiet. Orders from much higher up than base officials demanded that there be no unauthorized disclosure of the possibility that extraterrestrials had actually been recovered from the crash site, so the Army was free to be very harsh with witnesses. Even if one of the special personnel in intelligence or counterintelligence believed that a person had learned about what had happened, that person was dealt with as a potential threat, treated as a hostile, and given a dire warning about speaking to anyone about what he or she had seen. Even today, over sixty years after the Roswell incident, living witnesses are still afraid to come forward.

THE INTERNATIONAL UFO MUSEUM AND THE ROSWELL ANNIVERSARY CELEBRATIONS
The International UFO Museum and Research Center, founded by the late Walter Haut, the Army Air Force public information officer who first gave the press the report that the Army had pulled a flying saucer out of the desert, is open year-round and has lectures to accompany its video exhibits. Visitors can also get tours of the different suspected landing spots where they can look for their own Roswell debris. The city is home to many hotels, and the hospitality industry has grown in response to the large crowds that visit the city every year.

NO WORD FROM ARMY WITNESSES

The late staff sergeant Earl Fulford, who did tell his story of the debris field to Carey and Schmitt and who appeared as a witness on *UFO Hunters* to walk the television cameras across the debris field outside of Roswell, did his best to get other witnesses to come forward. Fulford knew much more about the Army's involvement—and the consequences for loose-lipped soldiers—than other willing witnesses. He revealed for the first time that Army personnel sitting outside on the hot New Mexico July nights actually saw UFOs over the base days before the reported crash. Personnel had observed at least two UFOs at the edge of the runway. However, they were told not to talk about the craft among themselves. After the crash and the cleanup of the debris field, the Army personnel involved in the cleanup were ordered on pain of severe punishment not to talk about their experience. Fulford contacted the truck driver who transported the crashed vehicle back to Roswell Army Airfield on an Army trailer and asked him to come forward to tell his story, but Fulford was not surprised when the veteran said no. And the answer was firm, too: "Sergeant, you know that orders are orders. And we were ordered not to talk about this. That's all I have to say."

CIVILIANS FEARED FOR THEIR LIVES

Sheriff George Wilcox and funeral home director Glenn Dennis were close friends in Roswell in 1947. Dennis reported that the Army warned Wilcox not to talk about the incident, promising him a very severe punishment if he came forward. In fact, the Army officers told the sheriff that if he dared speak about the crash openly, he and his entire family would simply disappear as if they had never existed. They would be taken out to the desert and left there for the vultures. Dennis said that when he and Wilcox wanted to talk about what happened, they would drive out to the desert until they were out of sight and out of earshot because they were so afraid of what the military would do to them.

NOT-SO-CONVINCING LIES

For a large number of researchers, Roswell is about more than what crashed out in the desert: it's about the cover-up. And we know it's been a cover-up because the government itself admitted it. In fact, they admitted it twice for *two* different cover-ups.

In the days after the crash and the subsequent retrieval—after Colonel Blanchard ordered Lieutenant Walter Haut to reveal the Roswell crash, after 509th intelligence officer Major Jesse Marcel flew the retrieved debris to Fort Worth—Army Air Force general Roger Ramey ordered Marcel to pose for cameras with debris from a weather balloon and retract the identification of the debris as alien. Yet over forty years later, in response to a query raised by the late Congressman Steven Schiff, the Army admitted that it had lied about the weather balloon—for national security purposes. Of course, they didn't admit that the debris was alien: Army officials said that the recovered debris came from a device called "Project Mogul," a top-secret radiation sensing device suspended from a balloon. The story became even more convoluted when the Army attempted to address reports of recovered alien beings.

In 1997 at the fiftieth anniversary celebration of the Roswell crash, the Air Force released another document explaining that Project Mogul wasn't the only operation allegedly taking place in 1947; a second operation apparently involving crash dummies gave rise to the stories about recovered extraterrestrials. The dummies might have looked like space aliens, but witnesses, they said, were clearly mistaken. The story sounds plausible enough, so why had not the Army or the Air Force come out with this story in July 1947? A simple answer: they hadn't thought of it yet. Why not? An even better answer: the military hadn't begun using crash dummies until 1950. Therefore, the 1997 cover-up was so obviously untrue that UFO researchers only laughed.

SECRETS FROM THE GRAVE

In *Witness to Roswell*, authors Carey and Schmitt disclose that in his later years, Army Air Force lieutenant Walter Haut changed his story. For over fifty years he had told anyone who asked him that he was only following orders when he released the flying saucer statement to the newspapers and had not seen anything strange himself, but near the end of his life Haut finally began to let it slip that he had, in fact, seen alien bodies. This was an astounding revelation because Haut had been the guardian of his commanding officer's weather-balloon legacy. It got easier for him to continue the lie in 1997 because when the Air Force released the Project Mogul explanation, Haut was relieved of his promise of silence and could talk about the balloon incident in greater detail. But even that wasn't the truth.

After 2000, Haut began to reveal the real story. He told a visiting press crew from France that he had seen alien bodies at Roswell. He also told a group of senior citizens who visited the International UFO Museum and Research Center—a museum that Haut himself had founded—that he had been to the crash site of an alien space ship and not a weather balloon or Project Mogul. And finally, he told documentary videographers Dennis Balthaser and Wendy Connor that a spacecraft crashed at Roswell, that he had seen it, and that he had seen an alien body covered up on a stretcher.

LIEUTENANT WALTER HAUT, IN UNIFORM (LEFT) AND IN 2004 (ABOVE)

In light of these disclosures, Carey and Schmitt asked Haut to tell the full story. It turned out that Haut had given an oath to his former boss Blanchard that he would guard the secrets throughout his life. Schmitt suggested that Haut tell the truth in a deathbed affidavit, a sworn statement made with the help of his lawyer and a notary public in contemplation of death. Such a statement has strong evidentiary value, but would allow Haut to keep his promise. And this is exactly what he did.

According to Carey and Schmitt, Haut swore out the affidavit in 2002 and ordered that it not be released until after his death; even then it would only be opened upon the sole and exclusive approval of his family. Haut died in 2005, and it wasn't until the publication of *Witness to Roswell* that his affidavit appeared in print for the first time.

The statement was nothing less than a bombshell. Haut completely reversed a lifetime of lies about what he knew, what he saw, and what he did. He said that not only was he informed that an extraterrestrial craft crashed at Roswell, he also visited the crash site, handled the extraterrestrial debris, saw the craft stored in the hangar at the Roswell Army Airfield base, and actually saw the alien creature covered up on a stretcher. He said that his boss indicated that the creatures were only about four-and-a-half-feet tall. He also tried to keep a piece of the alien spacecraft as a souvenir on his desk, but it was taken away and sent along with rest of the material to Fort Worth, Texas.

Haut's affidavit—and we must assume, if only for the sake of argument, that it was truthful—was a paradigm changing document. After almost sixty years, UFO researchers and Roswell scholars had a document that essentially validated everything that they had tried to argue over the decades. All skeptics and debunkers could do to decry the Roswell incident was argue Haut's credibility.

THE COVER-UP DETAILED

To researchers' delight, Haut's affidavit also described the process and methodology of the cover-up, and explained for the first time who was involved in its execution, how it destroyed Major Jesse Marcel's career, and ultimately drove Haut out of the Army Air Force.

The cover-up, it turns out, started long before Major Jesse Marcel was forced to change his story. Even though Haut's press release went to the newspapers citing July 8 as the official admission that the Army had recovered a flying saucer, General Roger Ramey and his aide Colonel Thomas Dubose flew to Roswell on July 7, where they were part of a meeting of the key officers from the 509th concerning the Roswell crash. Haut reveals that Ramey described two Roswell crashes: one forty miles out of the city and the other seventy-five miles out of the city. The public already knew about the first crash, Ramey said, but they didn't know about the second crash. The strategy for the hush-up: the Army would admit the first incident was the crash of a flying saucer, but reveal nothing about the second crash. All the officers around the table—including Haut, Colonel

GENERAL ROGER RAMEY

Blanchard, Marcel and Captain Sheridan Cavitt of the base CIC unit who had both been to the crash site, Colonel Thomas Dubose, and General Roger Ramey—agreed to the initial cover-up.

As planned, Marcel flew the debris to Ramey's headquarters in Fort Worth to make an expected public announcement about flying saucers to a group of assembled reporters, while Blanchard ordered Haut to deliver the press release to the media. However, at Fort Worth,

Ramey went off script. He covered up his own cover-up by switching the flying saucer crash wreckage with debris from a weather balloon and ordered Marcel to pose sheepishly with the weather balloon debris. Ramey had made Marcel the fall-guy for the entire cover-up. Haut believed Captain Cavitt was spared because he wasn't senior enough to have started such an uproar. And Blanchard had to be spared because he was complicit in Marcel's ousting; Ramey would not step into Blanchard's command structure without the base commander's okay. Haut was spared because he was too closely attached to Blanchard.

Though Marcel was ultimately promoted to lieutenant colonel, he had become embittered by the experience. Haut disclosed that Marcel absolutely refused to talk about what happened at Fort Worth. Jesse Marcel, Jr., has said that when his father came back from Fort Worth he told the family that they would not be allowed to talk about the Roswell incident ever again. Ultimately, Marcel decided to leave the Air Force after war broke out in Korea two years later and became a television repairman in Houma, Louisiana. All the while the true story of what happened at Roswell and his own role in the cover-up were eating at him.

WHAT TO DO IN ROSWELL, NEW MEXICO

There are plenty of other attractions in Roswell besides the festivals including, of course, museums, exhibits, and the monument to the father of American rocketry, Robert Goddard.

International UFO Museum and Research Center
114 North Main Street
Roswell, New Mexico

Roswell Museum and Art Center
100 West 11th Street
Roswell, New Mexico

In 1978, Marcel began telling his true story in public, denouncing the government's cover story about Roswell. Around that same time, nuclear physicist Stanton Friedman was also making appearances to talk about the mystery surrounding the discrepancy in the government's Roswell story and stories he had heard from folks who lived there in 1947. A radio talk show host put Friedman and Marcel together, and Friedman gained a first-hand eyewitness whose story could be presented as evidence of a cover-up. Marcel, also, had found an author who could tell the story of what really happened. Together, they began the first phase of Roswell disclosure.

As much as he was spared immediate shame, Haut's career was significantly altered by the cover-up. Those who knew Haut say that he might have risen through the ranks to a full colonel, serving as Blanchard's aide as the senior officer rose through the ranks to become the Air Force vice chief of staff. It is even possible that Haut could have made general. But Haut began to fear that a higher-ranking officer would one day order him to break his vow of silence, and as much as the cover-up ate at him, Haut's devotion was stronger. He left the Air Force to escape the possibility of such an ethical clash and remained in the small town of Roswell. He traded a brilliant military career to become an insurance broker and start the Roswell International UFO Museum. The museum at least, allowed Haut to give visitors all the evidence they wanted and to make their own opinions without ever giving them the real bombshell evidence that he knew in his own heart, all without breaking his promise to Blanchard.

ONCE COLONEL—NOW GENERAL— "BUTCH" BLANCHARD

CONSEQUENCES

The Roswell incident created more than just a favorite American legend. The subsequent cover-up destroyed two promising military careers and impacted hundreds and hundreds of lives—both military and civilian—through misinformation and threats of terrifying consequences. And while Haut's testimony went a long way to reveal buried secrets, the full truth still remains untold.

▶ UFO EVENTS

Roswell is the most important place destination for UFO enthusiasts, and many people bring their families to visit on Independence Day weekend to witness the goings-on. Many folks come back year after year because the events change as more witnesses come forward. The city hosts not one but two celebrations every July. At each event—one sponsored by the town and the other by the International UFO Museum—there are speakers, events, witnesses telling their stories, and reports on research done by the Roswell crash investigators.

The event draws authors like Whitley Strieber, Stanton Friedman, Tom Carey, and Don Schmitt. The UFO festival even launched Colonel Philip Corso's *New York Times* bestseller *The Day After Roswell* (1997) as well as Carey's and Schmitt's *Witness to Roswell*. Stanton Friedman—perhaps the most celebrated Roswell author and widely reputed to be the most important expert in the field—is a yearly guest at the anniversary celebration, sitting on panels with Roswell witnesses, much to the delight of annual visitors.

The Roswell UFO anniversary festival probably has the largest attendance of any UFO event in America, and takes place in the town where the history of modern UFO events in the United States began.

▶ PLACES TO STAY

If you're traveling to Roswell for the Roswell anniversary celebrations, you should know that hotels in town fill up fast. Here is the list of the hotels closest to the action during the festival:

Best Western El Rancho Palacio
2205 North Main Street
Roswell, New Mexico

Best Western Sally Port Inn & Suites
2000 North Main Street
Roswell, New Mexico

Candlewood Suites
4 Military Heights Drive
Roswell, New Mexico

Comfort Inn
3595 North Main Street
Roswell, New Mexico

Days Inn Roswell
1310 North Main Street
Roswell, New Mexico

Fairfield Inn & Suites Roswell
1201 North Main Street
Roswell, New Mexico

▶ PLACES TO STAY—continued

Hampton Inn and Suites Roswell
3607 North Main Street
Roswell, New Mexico

Holiday Inn Express Roswell
2300 North Main Street
Roswell, New Mexico

La Quinta Inn & Suites Roswell
200 East 19th Street
Roswell, New Mexico

Leisure Inn
2700 West Second Street
Roswell, New Mexico

Super 8 Roswell
3575 North Main Street
Roswell, New Mexico

Western Inn
2331 North Main Street
Roswell, New Mexico

Roswell is not a large city, and it's easy to walk to and from hotels, the exhibits, the events, and the museums. Many folks, however, visit Roswell in RVs and campers and for them there is also plenty of space.

Red Barn RV Park
2806 East Second Street
Roswell, New Mexico

Town & Country RV and Mobile Home Park
331 West Brasher Road
Roswell, New Mexico

▶ RESTAURANTS

There are plenty of fast food places in town, but the restaurants in town welcome festival visitors. Roswell is in the center of New Mexico's dairy and beef country, and if you like steak, this is the place to enjoy it.

The Cattle Baron
901 South Main Street #A
Roswell, New Mexico

The Cattleman's Steakhouse
2010 South Main Street
Roswell, New Mexico

Chew's West Restaurant
2509 West 2nd Street
Roswell, New Mexico

The Cowboy Café
1120 East 2nd Street
Roswell, New Mexico

▶ RESTAURANTS—continued

Martin's Capitol Café
110 West 4th Street
Roswell, New Mexico

Portofino Italian Restaurant
701 South Main Street
Roswell, New Mexico

Tia Juana's Mexican Grill & Cantina
3601 North Main Street
Roswell, New Mexico

Peppers Grill & Bar
500 North Main
Roswell, New Mexico

Billy Ray's
118 East 3rd Street
Roswell, New Mexico

Farley's Food, Fun, & Pub
1315 North Main Street
Roswell, New Mexico

Fat's Burritos
704 North Virginia Avenue
Roswell, New Mexico

Hunan
2609 1/2 North Main Street
Roswell, New Mexico

Hungry American Restaurant
3012 North Main Street
Roswell, New Mexico

Kaleidoscoops
910 A West Hobbs Street
Roswell, New Mexico

Phillip's Kountry Kettle
5800 South Main Street
Roswell, New Mexico

There are also coffee shops and sweet shops, sandwich shops, and two, count'em, two Starbucks.

CHAPTER FIFTEEN
WRIGHT FIELD AND THE MAC MAGRUDER STORY

DAYTON, OHIO

PUTTING ROSWELL AND THE COVER-UP INTO CONTEXT

Some of the answers, it seems, about the government's motivation to cover-up the truth about the Roswell Incident lie in what happened to the recovered UFO material transported from Roswell to Fort Worth and to Wright Field in Dayton, Ohio, in July 1947.

It is believed that the director of the Air Materiel Command at Wright Field, General Nathan Twining, was in the loop after the Army recovered the flying saucer. Various memoranda have finally surfaced to support this theory—including the now-famous note from Twining to General Schlugen dated September 23, 1947, in which General Twining says about flying saucers, "The phenomenon reported is something real and not visionary or fictitious." And as early as July 17, 1947, the CIA convened an Intelligence Advisory Board on UFOs and has since indicated that the flying saucer phenomenon is real and not fictitious.

Clearly, by the summer of 1947, the United States government was confronted with something its own internal memos from the military indicate that it did not understand. Their worst fears, it seemed, were on their doorstep.

THE U.S. GOVERNMENT'S BOGEYMEN

Something worried officials in the military and intelligence agencies enough to move quickly after the Roswell crashes. Perhaps military personnel were shaken by the possibility that the Soviets, who had gotten their hands on German rocketry materiel at the end of World War II, had developed some superior technology. Declassified FBI and intelligence documents from as far back as 1946 reveal that our government was terrified at the prospect of a KGB or GRU sleeper cell smuggling a small nuclear device over the U.S. border to set it off. Based on KGB files released after the Soviet Union collapsed, we now know that the KGB had scores of such sleeper cells ready to perpetrate acts of sabotage inside the United States. When the fear of sleeper cells' potential is paired with proof that sleeper cells existed, it makes sense to assume that the Army considered that debris retrieved from Roswell may well have been the remains of a vehicle for carrying a nuclear device.

Or perhaps the Japanese had some secret weapon that they had launched at the end of the war that was just now reaching the American southwest. Or maybe the mythological Foo Fighters that appeared over Germany during the Allied bombing raids were not mythological at all. Were they were real and controlled by an otherworldly intelligence? And what if that otherworldly intelligence was not just observing humans on earth but was actually in league with the Soviets?

> **HOW TO GET TO DAYTON BY AIR**
> Flights on all major airlines service Dayton International Airport (DAY) in Vandalia, right outside of Dayton.

And Roswell wasn't the first sighting that had the government worried. Experienced pilot Kenneth Arnold spotted a formation of flying crescent-shaped objects over Mount Rainer in Washington just weeks before the crash at Roswell. And some strange boatman in Puget Sound spotted a formation of six circular doughnut-shaped objects over Maury Island days before that. These sightings may have had something to do with the crash at Roswell. If so, then American air space security was seriously at risk, even if the intruders were extraterrestrials. In any case, the Air Force had plenty to worry about. They believed it best to keep Roswell a secret from the public until the military knew more about the possible threat and how to handle it.

> **RELATED SIGHTING**
> Read more about the Maury Island Incident in Chapter 18!

A PLAN

The Roswell Incident, therefore, inspired more than a cover-up: it influenced the military to develop policy for UFO sightings and crashes. And where better to develop that policy while examining the strange debris than at the Air Materiel Command at Wright Field outside of Dayton? And who better to take charge of the debris than General Nathan Twining, head of the Air Materiel Command? And what better group to call upon for advice in policy development than the young National Air War College officers soon to be promoted to senior command? That was the plan.

> **THE BEST MAN FOR THE JOB**
> Twining was the same man the federal government trusted with Professor Nikola Tesla's top-secret notes on antigravity and devices he was planning to develop for the Soviet Union at the outset of World War II. Heading up UFOs was a logical next step!

One of those officers at the National Air War College was Marine Lieutenant Colonel Marion Magruder, nicknamed "Black Mac" after the air combat techniques he brought to the Marines during the latter half of World War II. Trained in radar-vectored night fighting by the RAF—whose night fighting techniques won the Battle of Britain against the German Luftwaffe—Mac Magruder shared his skills with his Marine squadron and deployed them in the Pacific. In the especially bloody engagement at the battle off Okinawa, Magruder's Corsair squadron VMF (N) 533, called "Black Mac's Killers," successfully defended the Navy's carrier battle group and destroyers against kamikaze attacks launched by the enemy. In a brutal hand-to-hand engagement with suicide bombers who landed on the airfield where Magruder's squadron was stationed, Magruder and his men fought off the Japanese raiders.

Magruder was just one of the highly decorated and revered members of the Air War College's class of 1948 that was sent to Wright Field in 1947 for a very important observation. On his deathbed, he told his children that his class was tasked with helping the higher-ups in the military chain of command develop a policy concerning the material retrieved at Roswell, including the alien itself. The issue at hand: whether the military should disclose to the public the existence of extraterrestrials.

LIEUTENANT COLONEL MARION "BLACK MAC" MAGRUDER AND HIS PLANE "LIL MAC"

THE SPOILS OF ROSWELL

In July 1947, Magruder and his classmates were taken into a room at Wright Field where they were briefed about the crash at Roswell.

MAGRUDER IN HIS COCKPIT

They were shown physical debris from the crash—giving the lie to General Twining's statement to General Schulgen that the Air Materiel Command lacked "physical evidence" to prove the existence of flying saucers. Although one commentator has suggested that Twining might have been aware of the lack of security regarding his memo and therefore held back the facts that the Air Materiel Command had physical evidence, that would have been a stretch.

The young officers were asked to examine the material and the complete story of the Roswell crash. Shown photos of the object, they remarked that the object looked more like a disk than a triangle or a crescent. Magruder said that they were shown beams from the craft and he remembered that they had strange lettering or inscriptions on them. Jesse Marcel, Jr., Major Marcel's son, also handled some of the beams that his father brought home from the crash site on his way back to the base; he, too, said that he noticed strange inscriptions on the metallic objects. Magruder asked if the lettering on the beams had been translated into English, but the officers showing him the material had no answers. And then the members of Magruder's class were told that there was one more thing to see.

They were ushered into a room where, Magruder told his children, they came face to face with one of the inhabitants of the craft, the only one still alive after the crash. Magruder remembered that he just stared at the entity, looking directly into its face. He told his

A RADAR STATION AS IT MIGHT HAVE LOOKED IN 1952

children decades later that this was not like the creature "you see depicted on television." Not at all. Except for the large head, he said to his children, it actually looked human. "Instead of a gray color," Magruder said, "the being had a flesh tone."

The creature had a large head and large eyes, larger than a human, no protruding nose to speak of, and no real mouth that could be used for speaking or eating. Nevertheless, it resembled a human in shape. Magruder remembered the way it moved, the way it seemed to sway as it stared at the human faces gazing at it in awe. Magruder remarked that the creature's arms were overly long, longer proportionally than those of a typical human being. The fact that it was only four to four-and-a-half feet tall with exceptionally long swaying arms gave Magruder an eerie feeling. It was more human than not, and yet anyone looking at the creature knew it was not human. And that made it more frightening than any movie monster.

Magruder focused on the creature's undulating motion and long spaghetti-like arms. It reminded him of a jellyfish, he said, and he called the creature "Squiggly." Squiggly, he told his children, communicated with him. Not with words, Magruder explained, but by emotion or telepathy. He got the impression from the creature that it was telling them—

> **A RESTRICTED WELCOME AT WRIGHT-PATTERSON**
> Although formal tours of the base are not open to civilians, if your child is involved in Boy Scouts, Girl Scouts, or Air Explorers, the base's Scout Coordinator can arrange for Scout encampments on the base. ROTC, Junior ROTC, and Civil Air Patrol groups are welcome to visit the base. Requests for visits should be sent to the Outreach Division.

the Army Air Force—that the experiments they were conducting were harmful and that he was dying. "They're killing me," the creature communicated to Magruder. And Magruder told his children that he believed the entity was one of God's creatures. "It was alive," he said. "And we killed it." In the final years of his life, Magruder repeatedly told his children that: "It was a shameful thing that the military did to this creature by conducting tests on it that killed it."

Magruder's revelations about his contact with the creature from the Roswell craft and the crash debris at Wright Field comported with what others have said about the entities in the Roswell craft. A firefighter from Roswell and a handyman at the 509th Roswell Army Air Field, also called Walker Field, both described the entity that Magruder saw in similar ways. The handyman told his daughter as he was dying of cancer that when the creature he saw lying on a stretcher being carried into the hangar at Walker Field looked up at him, he knew that it was dying. He said that the creature was a pinkish color and that it reminded him of an insect found in the southwestern deserts called a "Child of the Earth." Like the other witnesses who came into direct contact with the extraterrestrial survivors of the Roswell crash, Magruder never forgot what he saw.

LIFE OF A SECRET-KEEPER

Years later, after having spent time at NATO Headquarters in Europe and serving on Eisenhower's staff, Magruder would find himself once again drawn into the controversy over UFOs. In July 1952, his youngest son said in an interview with *UFO Magazine*, his father was picked up at night in a black car and taken to the Pentagon. His son would find out later that Magruder was part of a crew listening in on conversations between Air Force pilots as they scrambled to intercept the flying saucers over Washington. Magruder heard the pilots announce that they had radar locks on the strange craft and reveal that the craft had managed to break the locks when they sped away. For two weekends this went on until the formation of flying saucers left the skies over the nation's capital.

AFB FUN FOR CIVILIANS, TOO The National Museum of the U.S. Air Force is adjacent to Wright-Patterson and is open to all visitors. If you're planning a vacation or driving through Ohio, the museum is a great weekend stop for any UFO enthusiast or tourist.

After he left the Marines, Magruder became a businessman and a McDonald's restaurant franchise owner. And twice a year, a pair of military officers—sometimes in uniform, sometimes in civilian clothes—would show up at the Magruder house to talk to the former pilot, asking him whether he had ever revealed the secret and to whom he might have revealed it. And twice every year Magruder gave the same answer. He had told no one; the secret was safe with him.

One night, his son remembers, as they were watching a television movie about the crash at Roswell, Magruder turned to his son and, out of nowhere, said, "Roswell was real. I know it." And then sank back into silence and wouldn't explain what he said. On another occasion, when his youngest son was watching the launch of a space shuttle and asked him if he thought there was life out there in the universe, Magruder told him, "There is, and I know that for a fact." But again, he wouldn't explain his answer.

It was only as he was slowly dying that he revealed the truth.

IN THE YEARS AFTER ROSWELL

The Roswell debris remained at Wright Field for study. The alien body was transported from Ohio to Walter Reed Army Hospital where it was autopsied. The autopsy results and some of the debris finally found their way into the Pentagon where they remained until 1961 when Lieutenant Colonel Philip Corso, then the director of foreign technology at Army R&D, worked with U.S. defense contractors to reverse engineer the wreckage into technologies for the military. The recovered Roswell craft and others that had been retrieved from subsequent crashes were ultimately sent to aerospace defense contractors and secure facilities. Some of the craft were sent to Area 51 for further study of their propulsion systems. Still others went to Lockheed Skunk Works. And still others might have found their way to the Army's Dugway Proving Ground in Utah. But over sixty years ago, the debris was first seriously studied at Wright Field in Dayton, a facility we know today as Wright-Patterson Air Force Base.

▶ PLACES TO STAY

Wright-Patterson is surrounded by the cities of Dayton, Vandalia, Kettering, and West Carrollton. There are plenty of hotels and motels in the immediate area, including:

Comfort Suites Wright-Patterson
5220 Huberville Avenue
Dayton, Ohio

The Dayton Marriott
1414 South Patterson Boulevard
Dayton, Ohio

The Dayton Crowne Plaza Hotel
33 East Fifth Street
Dayton, Ohio

**The Holiday Inn Express in Dayton/
Centerville**
5655 Wilmington Pike
Centerville, Ohio

▶ RESTAURANTS

Winds Café
215 Xenia Avenue
Yellow Springs, Ohio

The Paragon Supper Club
797 Miamisburg-Centerville Road
Washington Township, Ohio

Christopher's Restaurant
2318 East Dorothy Lane
Kettering, Ohio

Carvers Steaks & Chops
1535 Miamisburg-Centerville Road
Dayton, Ohio

Ajanta Indian Restaurant
3063 Woodman Drive
Dayton, Ohio

The Oakwood Club
2414 Far Hills Avenue
Dayton, Ohio

Mama DiSalvo's Ristorante
1375 East Stroop Road
Kettering, Ohio

CHAPTER SIXTEEN
THE PHOENIX LIGHTS

SOMETHING IN THE SKY

On March 13, 1997, shortly before seven in the evening, a witness in Henderson, Nevada spotted a large floating V in the air, larger than a Boeing 747, that had an arrangement of six lights along its leading edges. The object, seen by thousands of others that night, was described alternatively as flying wedge, a flying arrowhead, or a flying triangle. The Nevada witness said the lights were traveling toward the southeast, toward the Arizona border.

About twenty minutes after the Nevada sighting, a witness in Paulden, Arizona, said he saw a configuration of lights as well: four red-orange lights in a V-shaped formation heading toward him as he drove north. They moved slowly as they approached; as he reached his house, he watched as the lights disappeared off to the south.

Then, between 8:15 and 8:20 P.M., residents in the Prescott Valley area of Arizona—about ninety miles north of Phoenix—began reporting not only a V-shaped formation of lights, but an actual object in the sky. Witnesses said they could see the organized configuration of lights passing overhead and hear a soft rushing noise. The lights were traveling so slowly and so low to the ground that as they passed over rooftops, residents on upper balconies could make out a shape connecting the lights, a rigid structure that blocked out the stars. Some people said that they didn't see an object, per se, but a black shape that obstructed starlight definitely passed overhead. When the shape passed, the stars were visible again. Witnesses said they were sure they were seeing an object and not just a formation of disconnected lights.

Still other witnesses said that they could see an actual texture to the object. Witness Terry Mansfield reported that she and her friends

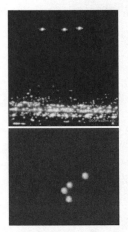

were meeting about local public school issues when one of them looked out the balcony windows to see the formation of lights off in the distance. She alerted the others, who went out onto the balcony and were awe-struck as a huge craft seemed to float directly at them. The witnesses said that the whole group fell silent as it glided effortlessly over rooftops. It was actually below the tips of the hilltops surrounding Prescott Valley, moving toward clusters of houses from the northwest to the southeast. The group on Mansfield's balcony said nothing to each other, as if the size of the craft and its gliding, noiseless appearance threw a blanket of wonder over them all.

LIGHT FORMATIONS OVER PHOENIX, ARIZONA BY AREA RESIDENTS

As it got closer, more than one witness said that she remembered thinking that if she had had a rock or any item to throw, she could have actually bounced it off the surface of the object—it was that close. A member of Mansfield's group said that she had the impression that if she had wanted to touch it, climb out over the gate on the balcony and reach up into the sky, she could have slid her hand along its shiny surface.

Still others on their respective balconies in this valley and hilltop community could observe other aspects to the object as it floated over. One person said that she noticed that the object had a "wavy" surface.

Another said that it was "shiny black." And still another was fascinated by what she called the object's "satin" surface that seemed to undulate softly as it floated over. It made no noise, yet it was so huge—blotting out the sky from hilltop to hilltop as lights from the houses below played off its bright diamond black texture—that everyone looking at it stood there as if in a trance.

IN SILENCE AND AWE

None of the witnesses in Terry Mansfield's house that night said anything to each other as it passed over. They were all overcome by what she called the majesty of the object and its beauty. In fact, the object seemed to impose a kind of a silence upon them, transfixing not only her small group of people standing on the balcony but, as she found out the next day from others who had watched the object pass by, stunning them into silence as well.

> **HOW TO GET TO PHOENIX BY CAR**
> By car from either east or west, take Interstate 10 right into the heart of Phoenix.

Strangely enough, this witness said, when she and her friends watched the object leave the area, they simply went back into her house and picked up where they left off at the meeting. There were no comments about the object, no conversation about what had just happened, and no phone calls out to other people. It was the strangest thing, she said, because one would think that an event of that magnitude would have prompted an extended conversation about its nature and what it all meant. But, when they went back into the room to continue their meeting, it was as if either by an unspoken agreement that every person ignored what had just happened or, alternatively, that the event had never taken place at all. And no one in the group had any sense of the passage of time. An hour could have gone by or two hours, but it was as if the time they spent watching the object had simply disappeared with their inclination to talk about the object. Was it something that had been imposed on them by the object itself or was it simply a group psychological reaction to the magnitude of the event?

THE ARIZONA GOVERNOR'S TALE

One prominent member of the Prescott/Phoenix witness group was Arizona governor Fife Symington. Symington has said in public interviews that he was driven home early that night and told his state police bodyguards that he was going straight to bed. Though he tried to sleep, something kept nagging at him to go out into his backyard. Normally, he would either stay in the house or have his bodyguards present if he were planning to walk around outside. But that night he had let them off. Something in the back of his mind convinced him to walk out into his backyard and take in the majesty of the night sky before turning in. And it was then that he saw it: the huge V-shaped formation of red-orange lights.

> **HOW TO GET TO PHOENIX BY AIR**
> Most major airlines fly into the Phoenix Sky Harbor International Airport (PHX), just outside of Tempe and minutes away along Interstate 10 from downtown Phoenix.

Symington said that when he was a lieutenant in the Air Force decades earlier, he had one anomalous radar target—a UFO. He reported it to his immediate superior officer, who noted what the young second lieutenant was telling him and told him point-blank to forget about it. Symington was not to report it because it never happened. And Symington did exactly what he was told and tucked it away as if it had never happened. But, in his own backyard decades later as the governor of Arizona, he watched an object that he clearly knew was not a conventional aircraft coming toward him. He, too, noted that the object was not just a formation of lights, but solid, and seemed to have a wavy surface through which he could see stars alternately appearing and disappearing. It was as if the surface, although solid, was sometimes translucent and sometimes not. It was nothing he had ever seen before in all his years in the Air Force and as a public servant. He watched as the object passed over his head, very close to the ground, and drifted off to the southeast. He, too, was overwhelmed by the size and apparent majestic appearance of the object.

As the object's effects wore off, Symington said he could see other people near his backyard also looking up at the sky as the object floated away. Some of them were talking about the object, but most of them were simply transfixed by an event far out of the paradigm of normal experience. Unlike many science fiction movies where the witnesses to flying saucers jabber among themselves about the presence of an unearthly object, this was the exact opposite. People seemed to

WHAT TO SEE IN PHOENIX

There are plenty of attractions in Phoenix for visitors wishing to see if strange lights are still occasionally visible in the night sky.

Arizona Science Center
600 East Washington Street in
Heritage and Science Park
Phoenix, Arizona

Desert Botanical Garden
1201 North Galvin Parkway
Phoenix, Arizona

Castles and Coasters
9445 Metro Parkway East
Phoenix, Arizona

Papago Park
625 North Galvin Parkway
Phoenix, Arizona

The Dodge Theater
400 West Washington Street
Phoenix, Arizona

Enchanted Island
1202 West Encanto Boulevard
Phoenix, Arizona

Casa Grande Ruins National Monument
1100 West Ruins Drive
Coolidge, Arizona

be either very private in their attempts to wrap their brains around what they were seeing or they were too privately overjoyed at having had the opportunity to witness something from beyond their experience to talk about it. Symington realized he had to find out what it was that he had just seen. He began making phone calls to public safety management officials and to the Arizona Air National Guard, a unit that he, as governor, technically commanded.

A SECOND WAVE

Thousands of residents saw the lights between 8:15 and 8:30 P.M. But the flap wasn't finished: there would be another appearance of lights just two hours later.

At about 10:30 that same evening, the lights were photographed by hundreds of people when they appeared in the skies over Prescott and Phoenix. These lights, according to some witnesses, were different from the lights affixed to a solid shape that appeared two hours earlier. Others claimed that they were the same exact reddish-orange lights that they had seen earlier. No matter the similarities or differences, when people realized that the lights were back, they grabbed their video cameras.

Both sets of lights prompted calls to 911 dispatchers, nearby Luke Air Force Base, and to the media. Folks wanted to know whether there were jets in the air from Luke, whether there were formations of helicopters in the air either from municipal police departments or from the sheriff, or whether the local news organizations were responsible for the heavy air traffic. Many of the Phoenix lights witnesses

TYPES OF FLARES

Witnesses often claim that they can recognize two basic types of flares blamed for UFO sightings:

- Ground illumination flares are dropped by several planes flying in patterns to light up an entire area.
- Chaff is released by individual jets, hangs in the air, and burns hot enough to draw away heat-seeking missiles.

were private or commercial pilots and retired Air Force pilots who were familiar with the patterns flares make when they are dropped. Many of them said that the 10:30 lights bore no resemblance to flares.

THE MEDIA TAKES IT SERIOUSLY

By the next day—March 14—the local and national media, even the syndicated gossip shows, were talking about the Phoenix lights. But unlike the news coverage in previous years that dismissed the witness reports as "tin hat claims," this media attention took the lights very seriously and marked a sea change in the way national media covered possible mass UFO sightings. The lights were not depicted as the precursor to Armageddon or linked to any other religious event.

One reason that the media and the Phoenix residents were especially interested in the night sky on March 13: it was during the time when the Hale-Bopp comet would be visible in the night skies. From February through April 1997—but especially in the middle of March—residents in the American southwest were on alert for the comet's appearance because it would have been one of the brightest objects in the sky. Instead, thousands of people looking for a comet saw the nation's most famous UFOs.

ANSWERS AND ALIBIS

By the end of the day on March 14, the Air National Guard—who initially had told Governor Symington and announced to the Phoenix residents that it had no planes in the air on the night of March 13—suddenly reversed its position on the previous night's events. It announced that units from the Maryland Air National Guard were engaged in "Operation Snow Bird" and were actually dropping flares from A-10 Warthogs over the Barry Goldwater test range at 10:30 P.M. This only fired up the debate about whether the second appearance of lights were flares or another set of objects. But it said nothing about the 8:30 P.M. set of lights.

Witnesses and the national media now fell into at least two separate camps. Skeptics took their lead from the Air National Guard and insisted that what folks had seen on March 13 at 10:30 P.M. were simply flares; there was no need to panic or create a storm of public interest. They, too, made no mention of the 8:30 lights, as if they were simply wishing them away. But another set of witnesses said that the 10:30 P.M. lights didn't match the color or the hover pattern of commonplace flares that many residents had seen the Air National Guard drop over the Barry Goldwater range.

The controversy lingered over the 10:30 P.M. lights for years. The Air National Guard eventually relented to witness demands for a flare test and to demonstrate that the 10:30 P.M. lights were clearly flares. But residents and researchers videotaped the flare drop and said that the new test only proved that the Air National Guard and the skeptics were wrong: the original lights photographed at 10:30 P.M. on March 13 were definitely not flares. Accordingly, although one can say that the issue of the 10:30 P.M. light sighting remains unresolved, others say that there were actually two sets of 10:30 P.M. lights. The Air National Guard may have attempted to provide a pretext for the whole event by staging a flare drop at 10:30 P.M. as the unidentifiable lights appeared, coordinating their operation to throw off residents from determining what they were seeing.

CONVINCING EVIDENCE—EVEN TO A SKEPTIC
Another key witness was Phoenix resident and physician Lynne Kitei, a self-described skeptic regarding UFOs. Until, of course, she saw the lights herself. Kitei's profession required that she find the causality of whatever symptoms her patients presented to her. Like the scientific

method—theory, testing, hypothesis, repeat independent testing to confirm the results—a medical model looks at symptoms, aligns them with a patient's presentation, performs testing and analysis, determines a diagnosis, and makes a differential diagnosis to separate the symptoms that might lead the diagnostician in the wrong direction. And this is exactly what Kitei began to do after she and thousands of other people saw the lights.

Kitei's research brought her to an epiphany as she analyzed her photos with the help of retired U.S. Navy physicist and CIA consultant Dr. Bruce Maccabee. Their analysis uncovered something strange. Upon investigating the photos, their negatives, and the different rolls of film, they realized that Kitei took more photos than she remembered. Maccabee suggested that Kitei had experienced a portion of missing time during which she took photos that she did not remember taking, but which photos she still had and served as proof that she was performing an activity that had dropped out of her memory. Kitei and Maccabee are still evaluating the nature and cause of that missing time, an experience several floating triangle witnesses have reported over the years.

NO LAUGHING MATTER
Governor Symington reported that he'd found out what caused the lights and ordered a press conference only to have his chief of staff appear in an ET costume. His effort to "lighten the mood" backfired; witnesses were furious. Years later, Symington apologized to his former constituents.

OURS, THEIRS, OR FLARES?

What were the Phoenix lights? Whether an extraterrestrial craft or some other kind of unconventional and otherworldly vehicle, the V-shaped or arrowhead-shaped triangular craft resembles the object seen and photographed seven years earlier over Belgium, and seen six years later over RAF Cosford in the United Kingdom. UFO researchers say they are still completely unexplained. Some military experts have suggested that flying triangles are actually very advanced and still top-secret neutral buoyancy aircraft that have a variety of stealth devices on them. They can cloak themselves so that the night sky seems to shine through them, they can move through the air invisibly by turning off their lights, they can project an image of themselves to make it seem as if they are taking off at hyper-mach speeds, and they can soar to extremely high altitudes so that they can traverse large distances in a matter of hours while transporting huge amounts of personnel and materiel. The debate about what the flying triangles are and the nature of the Phoenix lights is still wide open.

▶ UFO EVENTS

For those who want to meet Phoenix lights witnesses, it's not hard. Many of the witnesses like Dr. Lynne Kitei, have their own websites and give regular talks at conferences on the Phoenix lights. The Arizona MUFON chapter also conducts regular meetings about the Phoenix lights that are open to visitors.

▶ PLACES TO STAY

The Clarendon Hotel
401 West Clarendon Avenue
Phoenix, Arizona

The Hyatt Regency Phoenix
122 North Second Street
Phoenix, Arizona

The Holiday Inn Express
620 North 6th Street
Phoenix, Arizona

Arizona Biltmore
2400 East Missouri Avenue
Phoenix, Arizona

The Wyndham Phoenix
50 East Adams Street
Phoenix, Arizona

Doubletree Guest Suites Phoenix
320 North 44th Street
Phoenix, Arizona

Hampton Inn & Suites Phoenix/Tempe
1429 North Scottsdale Road
Tempe, Arizona

▶ RESTAURANTS

Portland's Restaurant and Wine Bar
105 West Portland Street
Phoenix, Arizona

Cibo
603 North 5th Avenue
Phoenix, Arizona

Alice Cooperstown
101 East Jackson Street
Phoenix, Arizona

Mac Alpine's Soda Fountain
2303 North 7th Street
Phoenix, Arizona

The Wrigley Mansion
2501 East Telawa Trail
Phoenix, Arizona

Aunt Chilada's Restaurant
7330 North Dreamy Draw Drive
Phoenix, Arizona

CHAPTER SEVENTEEN
1950s CONTACTEES AND THE INTEGRATRON

A CONVENIENT CULTURE OF DISMISSAL

There was an innocence in popular culture about the 1950s ET contactees. It was a time of wild speculation about the nature of the flying saucers that people saw in movie theater newsreels. Newspaper headlines about flying saucer sightings and landings abounded, and not just in the tabloid press. And it seemed that each week there was another great flying saucer movie such as *Invaders from Mars, The Day the Earth Stood Still, This Island Earth, It Came from Outer Space,* and *Earth vs. The Flying Saucers.* Movies like these whipped up the popular imagination and—even better for a government trying to grapple with the nature of flying saucers—turned what might have been a real threat to our airspace into pure fiction.

Anyone who claimed to have seen a UFO was relegated to the status of one of the self-proclaimed witnesses out of a science fiction movie. It lessened the perceived threat and bought the government valuable time in assessing what, if any, danger UFOs posed to the United States. This was particularly important in the immediate aftermath of the flying saucer invasion over Washington, DC. Whatever these things were, they could outrun our fastest jets, break the most advanced radar lock, and toy with our most powerful deterrents to their threats. Why were they here? What did they want? What could we do to protect ourselves? Imagine that you were President Harry Truman or President Dwight Eisenhower looking at the photos of these craft and hearing the reports of their invulnerability from your own military chiefs. It's not the news you want to get, especially with newspaper reporters clamoring for answers. Thank goodness, you might have said, for the stories coming out of the contactees.

THE CONTACTEE MOVEMENT

In the very late 1940s and right through the 1950s, a group of people—including George Adamski, George Van Tassel, Howard Menger, and Frank Stranges—revealed that not only did they know the true origins of the flying saucers folks were seeing in the skies, but they knew who piloted them, what they wanted, and what messages they had for humankind. The space aliens were actually our "space brothers:" tall and blonde with piercing blue eyes, benevolent but secure behind their invulnerability, and welcoming the people of earth to a galactic age.

> **ONE HOT, HISTORIC DRIVE**
> Landers is a scorching drive into the desert, where temperatures in the summer routinely spike over 120°F and at night dip into the 40s. It's a drive well worth taking from Los Angeles because the sight of the Integratron is a testament to the UFO and ET contact stories of the 1950s. Take Interstate 10 whether you're traveling from the East Coast or from LA.

According to Stranges, who met the alien Valiant Thor at the Pentagon, these creatures were able to appear and disappear at will, cloak themselves in invisibility, and pop inside the halls of power without causing a stir. According to Menger, they brought messages of peace and warnings that the people of the earth needed to keep from destroying each other and the planet. They even saved the life of Menger's son. And, oddly enough, even though we didn't know much about our neighboring planet in the solar system, these extraterrestrial aliens came from Venus.

How great it was to know that at a time of fast food restaurants popping up along the roadside like dandelions, of ice cream "flying saucers," and of rock 'n roll, that the contactees were telling us that real flying saucers were actually friendly and their inhabitants wanted to help us. As an homage to that age, Los Angeles architect Paul Williams designed the famous flying saucer dome at Los Angeles International Airport in 1961 and, although pieces of it have deteriorated in recent days, it still stands today as the symbol of an age.

GEORGE ADAMSKI

Adamski was one of the original and most celebrated UFO contactees of the 1950s. A very prolific author, he documented his claims of extraterrestrial contact in a series of books and articles. His work generated a following of enthusiasts who believed in the messages of peace he received from our neighboring planet and found his photographs of flying saucers to be tantalizingly real. Despite his claims and his impact on popular culture in the 1950s, Adamski was also derided as a hoaxer and cult figure who made false claims about his contact with "space brothers."

Adamski immigrated to the United States from Poland at the end of the nineteenth century. He led a very peripatetic life, moving from New York to the Mexican border as a trooper in the United States Cavalry, to Oregon as a mill worker, and ultimately to the hillside on Palomar Mountain in California. There he and a group of followers established a homestead and a busi-

HOW TO GET TO LANDERS BY AIR
Flying to the Landers area, you can land at Los Angeles International Airport (LAX) and take the four-hour drive to Landers. You can also fly into Bob Hope Airport (BUR) in Burbank, California, McCarran International Airport (LAS) in Las Vegas, Nevada, or Laughlin/ Bullhead International Airport (IFP) in Bullhead City, Arizona.

ness on land purchased for them by one of his students. Among his many professions, Adamski had also styled himself as a philosopher and a teacher.

It was on Palomar Mountain in October 1946, that Adamski and his followers claimed to have had their first major flying saucer sighting. The group saw a cigar-shaped craft during a meteor shower, and Adamski dubbed it the "mother ship." In 1947—the same year of the Roswell crash, the Kenneth Arnold sighting over Mount Rainer, and the Harold Dahl sighting on Maury Island, Washington—Adamski said he took a photograph of the mother ship, which became publicized as one of the first flying saucer photographs.

In 1950 and 1952, Adamski released more photographs of what he said were flying saucers, one of which was used by the nation of Grenada as a commemorative stamp depicting what it called "the year of the UFO." And in 1952, Adamski and his group were in the desert in Riverside County, California, when they spotted a huge tubular flying saucer in the sky. Adamski later said that he left the group to follow the ship, which descended and sent out a smaller craft to land near him. He said that the pilot of the craft, an extraterrestrial from Venus named Orthon, had been looking for him to warn him of the dangers of an impending nuclear war. It was a war that could be fatal to Earth. Adamski said that Orthon was blonde and well tanned and was able to use a form of sign language to communicate. He also projected his thoughts into Adamski's mind by mental telepathy.

> **VISITING THE INTEGRATRON AND THE GIANT ROCK**
>
> Like Roswell, the Integratron has become a pilgrimage location for UFO enthusiasts. The Giant Rock itself, only three miles north of the Integratron, is the largest freestanding boulder in the world at seven stories high. It is a sacred site for Native Americans as well as the place where George Van Tassel brought his family to live.

People asked why Adamski never photographed this creature since he had photographed UFOs; Adamski said that Orthon refused to pose for a photograph, suggesting instead that Adamski give him a photographic plate that he would expose himself. A month later, Orthon allegedly returned the photographic plate to Adamski, who said that the plate had exotic symbols on it. During that same month, Adamski released a photo of a flying saucer, which photo analysts later sought to debunk as a streetlight.

Critics notwithstanding, Adamski pursued his public revelations about his contacts with flying saucers and "space brothers" and his thoughts about the unity of life on other planets. His reputation grew to the point where, even as mainstream ufologists were deriding him as a wannabe cult leader, he was inspiring interest in his beliefs in Europe. Perhaps one of the highlights of his career was an invitation from Queen Juliana of the Netherlands to be her guest at court. At this 1959 meeting, according to statements from the Dutch Aeronautical Association, the Queen seemed to be fascinated by what Adamski had to say, including his stories of contact with extraterrestrial humanoids.

Among Adamski's many claims were descriptions of invitations from Orthon and the Venusians to climb aboard their spacecraft for a trip through the solar system and a visit to their home planet. Adamski also said that he had been invited to attend an interplanetary meeting on Saturn, and had met with Pope John XXIII to deliver messages from the Venusians.

DRIVING TO PALOMAR MOUNTAIN

From Los Angeles, take I-10 East to I-5 South to CA 60 East. CA 60 East to CA 71 South toward Corona and then follow signs to CA 91 East to I-15 South toward San Diego. Exit I-15 South at CA 79 South, Temecula Parkway. From CA 79 South make a right on Oak Grove Truck Trail. From Oak Grove Trail, make a left at High Point Truck Trail and take that to Palomar Dive Road and make a right to the mountain.

In his later years, Adamski suffered declining health even as he weathered the claims by skeptics and debunkers that he was a fraud who was hoaxing the public about his UFO contacts. Adamski died of a heart attack in April 1965, but he left a legacy of popular culture in the 1950s that remains to this day.

GEORGE VAN TASSEL

Out in the desert of Landers, California—the site of a very powerful earthquake along the San Andreas Fault on June 28, 1992—stands the Giant Rock where enigmatic self-described alien contactee George Van Tassel announced to the world that he had communicated with humanoid aliens from Venus in the 1950s. Like George Adamski, Van Tassel said that aliens had sought him out to convey their message to humankind.

Van Tassel's Integratron project began when he acquired a lease from the federal government to an area around a massive rock, a place that had been shown to him by a mining prospector. Van Tassel moved his family out to the rock in 1945 and began meditating in rooms he had dug under the rock. It was there, he said, that a space ship from Venus landed. Van Tassel told anyone who would listen to him that he was actually tutored, mentored, and instructed by the aliens on how to rejuvenate the human cellular structure. At a time twenty years before the concept of "pyramid power" had become popular, Van Tassel was given a detailed set of instructions to build a structure called the Integratron. It was a building, to be sure, but it was more of a vessel that was able to focus energy in such a way that the entire human cellular structure was said to be rejuvenated.

After he built the structure, Van Tassel and his family held conventions at the Giant Rock and the Integratron, telling willing guests and attendees how to stay young, full of energy, and healthy. Van Tassel launched a career as an author; his books detailed his conversations with the Venusians and the science behind time travel. After his death, the area around the Giant Rock was vandalized, but a group of Van Tassel's former disciples maintained the Integratron. To this day, they host tours of the facility and explain Van Tassel's message.

▶ UFO EVENTS

Scores of conventions are still held in Landers and the Giant Rock, commemorating Van Tassel's teachings and the science behind the construction of the Integratron. The meetings at Big Rock are also near the Joshua Tree area of California, a place where there are many assemblages of spiritual groups and meditative groups in the magnificent California desert.

▶ PLACES TO STAY

The Lonesome Dove Motel
1600 Old Woman Springs Road
Landers, California

Super 8 Yucca Valley and Joshua Tree
57096 29 Palms Highway
Yucca Valley, California

Joshua Tree Inn
61259 29 Palms Highway
Joshua Tree, California

▶ RESTAURANTS

Crossroads Café and Tavern
61715 29 Palms Highway
Joshua Tree, California

CHAPTER EIGHTEEN
THE MAURY ISLAND INCIDENT

KICKING OFF THE UFO ERA

On June 21, 1947—only three days before the famous Kenneth Arnold flying saucer sightings over Mount Rainier, Washington, and two weeks before the Roswell crash in New Mexico—Puget Sound salvage boatman Harold Dahl reported that he saw a formation of six circular craft, or what he called "flying doughnuts," shooting through the air over his boat. One of the craft, he said, seemed to be in trouble, wobbling from side to side as if it were unable to maintain its altitude. The other objects in the formation seemed to surround it as if to render it some kind of invisible aid. And then the wobbling object ejected a metallic substance, which Dahl referred to as a "slag," and the six objects flew off. The slag hit Dahl's boat, breaking his son's arm, killing his dog, and damaging the boat.

That was the essence of the story: a testimony that an object Dahl was unable to identify left trace evidence, damaged his boat, and harmed his son and pet. In the next three days, Dahl's sighting impressed him enough that he said he took photographs of the objects and retrieved some of the material that he said the troubled craft ejected. He referred to the substance as "slag," but said that it was a light malleable type of metal and not real slag—the glassy residue that usually floated over to Maury Island from the smelting plant across the channel in Tacoma. Despite the strangeness of his sighting, Dahl didn't report what he saw right away.

Adding to the strangeness—some researchers say the importance—of the event, the next morning, Dahl said with no real corroboration available, a person whom he assumed was from the military or a law enforcement agency showed up at his residence and invited him to breakfast. The man was wearing a dark suit, had an official and authoritative bearing, and repeated to Dahl the details of his sighting the day before. Dahl was surprised: he had not reported the event. The man advised Dahl that he make no public statement about what happened. He said Dahl should simply forget about it because if he disregarded this advice and started talking about this publicly, things would not go well for him and his family. While the stranger made no direct threats, the implication that Dahl took away from this conversation was that he and his family would be harmed. Ultimately, this was advice that Dahl did not take, but advice that would have inured well for him had he heeded it.

> **THE WHATCHAMACALLITS**
> When Dahl spotted the UFOs, the American public had never heard the words "flying saucer." The phrase was invented by the media to characterize the flight patterns of the crescent-shaped craft that Kenneth Arnold saw three days *after* the Maury Island Incident.

QUESTIONABLE CHARACTERS

At the time of the sighting, Dahl was operating a salvage boat owned by Fred Crisman; together they ran a business of retrieving logs that had fallen off of timber barges in Puget Sound and selling them back to the logging companies. Crisman, a wannabe intelligence operative who said he'd seen action in Burma during World War II, would be named by Jim Garrison sixteen years later in connection with Clay Shaw in the investigation into the John F. Kennedy assassination. Some have suggested that Crisman was one of the three tramps on the grassy knoll who were stopped and released. In the 1960s, Crisman was the host of his own radio talk show in Tacoma, broadcasting under the name of Jon Gold.

SUBTERRANEAN SIGHTINGS?

In 1946, Crisman—who fancied himself a writer—wrote to *Amazing Stories* saying that he believed there were demonic entities living under the earth who had attacked him with a beam weapon while he was fighting against the Japanese.

Because of his relationship with Crisman, Dahl only waited another day and then told his partner about the incident. Crisman took a boat out into Puget Sound to investigate the area himself. He said that he, too, saw one of Dahl's doughnut-shaped craft, but it disappeared before he could get a real good look. However, he said that he found some of the material that Dahl referred to as "slag" along the Maury Island beach; he retrieved and sent it to a researcher in Chicago for analysis. A comprehensive FBI report on this incident later indicated that there was some confusion over whether Crisman sent the slag samples to the University of Chicago or to his acquaintance Ray Palmer, publisher of the science fiction magazines *Fantasy and Science Fiction*, *Fate Magazine*, and *Amazing Stories*. Either way, ultimately Palmer learned of the story, a factor that would be critical in the next few days.

CONTEXT FROM MT. RAINIER

Two days after Dahl reported his story to Crisman, the Kenneth Arnold sighting made headlines. Pilot Kenneth Arnold, flying about sixty miles southeast of Maury Island, near Mount Rainier just before 3 P.M. in search of a missing Marine cargo plane, saw a series of bright flashes off to the side of his aircraft. He thought it was another plane at first and then he thought it might be a flock of birds. But the flashes were too high in the sky and flying too fast to be birds. Arnold got a better look at the source of the flashes and realized they were solid objects. He believed them to be test aircraft, possibly a new type of Air Force jet, but when he looked closer he saw that they had no tail assembly of any kind. To him, they did not look conventional at all. As the formation passed in front of him, some of the craft turned over on their sides, and Arnold marveled at their thinness. He said later that although the craft were generally circular, he could make out a clear crescent shape in one or two of them. He said they moved in a fluttering fashion as if someone were skipping a saucer across the surface of the water. And that was how the name "flying saucer" came into

PACIFIC NORTHWEST ISLAND CULTURE

After beachcombing, vacationers might want to enjoy some of the islands' cultural attractions.

Blue Heron Art Center
19704 Vashon Highway SW
Vashon Island, Washington

Gallery 070
17633 Vashon Highway SW
Vashon Island, Washington

Heron's Nest
17600 Vashon Highway SW
Vashon Island, Washington

Silverwood Gallery
23927 Vashon Highway SW
Vashon Island, Washington

Vashon Allied Arts
19704 Vashon Highway SW
Vashon Island, Washington

Point Robinson Lighthouse
SW Point Robinson Road and SW
Luana Beach Road
Vashon Island, Washington

Vashon Maury Island Heritage Association Museum
10105 Bank Road SW
Vashon Island, Washington

Drama Dock Community Theater
9919 SW 204th Street
Vashon Island, Washington

Vashon Theatre
17723 Vashon Highway
Vashon Island, Washington

existence. Arnold never used it himself, but a newspaper carrying the story of Arnold's sighting used it to describe what Arnold saw.

After Arnold reported what he saw to friends at the airport in Yakima and to other pilots, news of his sighting spread. It was covered in newspapers, and Arnold immediately became something of a celebrity—something he did not want. People who initially thought the whole thing was a delusion or a made-up story were stunned into silence when another witness, Fred Johnson, said he saw the same objects through his telescope while he was on Mount Adams. He reported that the objects had a similar shape and configuration and that he saw them at the same time Arnold made his sighting. Suddenly, flying saucers were in the news. In Fred Crisman's mind, it gave Harold Dahl's sighting a whole new significance.

THE INVESTIGATION BEGINS

Magazine publisher Ray Palmer was now in possession of the slag material, and suddenly saw an opportunity with the celebrity of Kenneth Arnold. Palmer wrote to Arnold and invited him to investigate the Harold Dahl sighting and the slag material Dahl and Crisman had recovered.

A FAMOUS DEBUT FOR A FAMOUS WITNESS
Ultimately Kenneth Arnold would write an article about his sighting for the first issue of Palmer's *Fate Magazine* in January 1948.

Arnold's investigation never turned up any corroborative evidence for Dahl's story. His inspection of the boat revealed that the boat had been recently painted and he couldn't find any evidence of burn marks or any structural damage to the areas along the deck where Dahl said the slag hit. Dahl's son had run away in the days since the sighting and was unable to confirm any of the story. Dahl was unable to locate the photographs he said he had taken.

Testing confirmed that the slag itself was a ferrous material, and no test results returned any unknown elements or especially exotic alloys of known elements. In short, all Arnold had to go on was Dahl's story.

Nevertheless, Dahl's story was investigated by Army Air Force intelligence thanks to Arnold's help. In particular, Lieutenant Frank Brown had interviewed Arnold and found him to be highly credible, a good family man, a professional observer because he was a pilot, and a person not given to any fantasy. Brown wrote a highly complimentary report on Arnold pursuant to Arnold's Mount Rainier sighting. Accordingly, when Arnold contacted Army Air Force intelligence to report Dahl's sighting, Lieutenant Brown became one of the investigators, largely on the basis of his confidence in Arnold's credibility.

HOW TO GET TO MAURY ISLAND AND VASHON ISLAND BY AIR
All major airlines service the Seattle-Tacoma (Sea-Tac) International Airport (SEA).

Crisman and Palmer pressed the slag material they had collected on Lieutenant Brown and his senior officer Captain William Davidson. Davidson and Brown had flown to Tacoma on a Mitchell B-25 bomber from the Hamilton Army Air Force base in California. They had to get back to Hamilton the next day, but after interviewing Dahl and Crisman and finding no other evidence to support Dahl's story besides the slag material, decided to fly it back to California for further testing. The pair, along with a flight sergeant and another sergeant on board, took off the next day but never made it back to California. A series of fires on board the B-25— including one in the bomb bay and another

HOW TO GET TO MAURY ISLAND AND VASHON ISLAND BY CAR
By car from points south take Interstate 5 to Tacoma or Seattle where you will find the Vashon Island ferry. From points east take Interstate 90 to Seattle and follow the signs to the Vashon Island ferry.

A UFOLOGOIST'S RETREAT

As a stop on a UFO sightseeing excursion, Maury and Vashon Islands, on Puget Sound, offer a great vacation. Easily reachable from the Sea-Tac airport in Seattle, Vashon Island offers some of the best bed and breakfast establishments in the Northwest. Nestled near the beach, these Victorian-style B&Bs offer home cooking, very comfortable rooms, and a relaxing scenic environment. The only comparable scenic setting on the East Coast is a trip to New England or Prince Edward Island in Canada for an Anne-of-Green-Gables experience. A vacation in warm weather, especially in early fall when Puget Sound is still relatively inviting, is worth the trip. And beachcombers can still find pieces of slag among the pebbles along the beach where Harold Dahl first sighted UFOs over sixty years ago.

along the wing in the left engine—caused pilots Davidson and Brown to lose control of the aircraft. They ordered the two sergeants to parachute out. Both jumped out over a desolate area in Kelso, Washington, and survived. Davidson and Brown, however, decided to try to bring the plane in for a landing. As the wing began to incinerate, they lost all control and crashed in Kelso. Both Davidson and Brown were killed.

At first, there were thoughts that the plane had been sabotaged, but an investigation by the *UFO Hunters* team in 2008 revealed that the highly ferrous nature of the slag material inside the bomb bay might have caused critical junction and relay boxes to overload. The resulting short circuit could have sent an electrical discharge to the junction and relay box at the left wing engine starting the fire that caused the plane to crash. The Army never determined the conclusive reason for the crash, saying only that it was due to a mechanical failure.

After the deaths of Davidson and Brown, the FBI became involved in the case. In an interview with Dahl, according to the FBI report, he admitted that the whole UFO sighting and slag collection was a complete hoax. He had made it up for publicity. Dahl's wife even blurted out that Dahl should confess to the FBI that this whole affair was a hoax. Dahl fully recanted his story.

Crisman dropped out of sight to become a teacher at Tacoma High School. Dahl later recanted his recantation, but the entire story of the Maury Island sighting and the Kelso crash drifted into UFO legend and lore, covered extensively by *UFO Magazine* and *Fate Magazine* as well as on a number of television documentaries, including *UFO Files* and *UFO Hunters*, both on the History Channel.

▶ PLACES TO STAY

A&E Bed and Breakfast
10910 SW 232nd Street
Vashon Island, Washington

Angels of the Sea Bed & Breakfast
26431 99th Avenue SW
Vashon Island, Washington

Casa Vista Bed & Breakfast
6700 Luana Beach Road
Vashon Island, Washington

Cove Haven
16805 137th Avenue SW
Vashon Island, Washington

Madrona Meadows Bed and Barn
21828 Monument Road SW
Vashon Island, Washington

Rambling Rose Bed & Beach
23109 Kingsbury Road SW
Vashon Island, Washington

Tramp Harbor Lookout
8016 SW 222nd Place
Vashon Island, Washington

Back Bay Inn
24007 Vashon Highway SW
Vashon Island, Washington

Vashon Island Inn
18522 Beall Road SW
Vashon Island, Washington

AYH Ranch Hostel
12119 SW Cove Road
Vashon Island, Washington

▶ RESTAURANTS

Back Bay Inn
24007 Vashon Highway SW
Vashon Island, Washington

Cafe Luna
9924 SW Bank Road
Vashon Island, Washington

The Hardware Store Restaurant
17601 Vashon Highway SW
Vashon Island, Washington

Red Bicycle Bistro & Sushi
17618 Vashon Highway SW
Vashon Island, Washington

Vashon Homegrown Café
17614 Vashon Highway SW
Vashon Island, Washington

Splash Seafood Bar & Market
17635 100th Avenue SW
Vashon Island, Washington

CHAPTER NINETEEN
THE TRENT PHOTOGRAPHS

PHOTOGRAPHIC FUEL FOR CONTROVERSY

In the history of the UFO phenomena in America, photographic evidence—like the photos taken by Ed Walters in Gulf Breeze, Dr. Lynne Kitei in Phoenix, and Paul Trent in McMinnville, Oregon—has been among the most controversial and the most analyzed proof.

You would think that a photo of a flying saucer or flying triangle would be the consummate proof of the existence of UFOs. But in the battle among scientists, skeptics, true believers, and debunkers, the debate over photographic evidence takes on not only the arcane metrics of light, shade, angles of sun, and proportionality of the photographic subject, but also the prejudices of those into whose hands the photos are delivered. In some cases, real or self-appointed government operatives—out of a sense of almost fanatic dedication to keeping the UFO secrets hidden—have simply destroyed photos, doctored them, or kept them out of the public eye for decades until the controversy has died down. But in the case of a few photos, the analysis arguing for their authenticity has survived the controversy. This is the case in the McMinnville photos taken by Paul Trent after his wife Evelyn spotted a strange disk-shaped object in the sky above their farm.

Even though the photos were compelling and very revealing, the actions of government agencies, debunkers, and the impact on the lives of the photographers were as equally expressive. One has to ask, why would the government and the debunkers go to such great lengths to destroy not only the photos, but the reputations of the photographers if there weren't something there to be destroyed in the first place?

A SILVERY THING ABOVE THE BARN

The McMinnville incident began on May 11, 1950 on the Trent family farm outside McMinnville, Oregon. Evelyn Trent saw a disk-shaped object that was maneuvering at strange angles to the ground, seemingly fading in and out of view as if it were materializing and dematerializing. She watched it, called out for her husband Paul to come outside to see the thing, and the two of them stared and wondered what it was. While the object was still in view, Paul ran back into the house, grabbed his camera, and came out to snap off two photos of the object before it flew away.

The Trents described the object as "silvery" with a bronze-like tone and saucer-shaped with a "parachute dome" on top. The object had no visible means of propulsion, emitted no flames or exhaust smoke, and made no noise. The photo analysts would later suggest that the object had a haze around it as if it were generating some type of magnetic field.

FROM SNAP SHOT TO ICON

The Trent photos of this object have become some of the most analyzed and debated photographs in the history of UFOs in America. Even photo analysts at the University of Colorado ultimately endorsed the photos.

Another factor weighing favorably for the Trents' credibility and the authenticity of the photos was their decision not to make the photos

Evidence from the uncovered Trent negatives

McMinnville, Oregon ■

public. In fact they sought no publicity whatsoever. They showed the photos to their banker in McMinnville—farmers and bank lenders are usually on very close terms—and the banker, Frank Wortmann, put them up in his front window. Evidently, Wortmann was so fascinated by the photos, in light of the national publicity surrounding the Kenneth Arnold sighting three years earlier, he wanted to show them off. From his window, the photos attracted immediate attention, virally spreading out beyond the small circle of the Trents' friends and associates.

A local reporter in the McMinnville area named Bill Powell saw the photos and became so interested in them that he asked to see the negatives. Had the photos been faked the contact negatives would tell more of a story than the prints. Powell's analysis of the negatives convinced him that whatever the Trents photographed was real. He published the Trents' story of their sighting and their photographs in the local paper, and the story was picked up by the International News Service (INS), and broadcast over their wire. The Trent sighting and photos quickly became international news.

The negatives traveled quite far from Powell's hands before the Trents were able to reclaim them. In July 1950, *Life Magazine* got their hands on the original film and published the photos, cementing the Trent story into popular culture. This was not what the Trents had wanted, and when they asked *Life* to send them back the negatives, the magazine told them that the negatives were lost.

AT THE MERCY OF SKEPTICS

Mysteriously, seventeen years later, the INS—which by then had become United Press International—discovered the negatives that *Life Magazine* said they had lost and turned them over to one of the

investigators at the University of Colorado on the newly formed Condon Committee. The Condon study was commissioned by the United
States Air Force for the express purpose of debunking the UFO phenomenon so as to allow the Air Force publicly to get out of the UFO
business by shutting down Project Blue Book. As a result of the debacle
in 1952 when the Air Force had to lie bold-faced to the American public about what everyone saw on the movie newsreels and newspaper
photos and in light of subsequent publications by former Blue Book
project director Captain Edward Ruppelt and
retired Marine Major Donald Keyhoe, the Air
Force was taking a beating. Why be in the UFO
public relations business when you can get out of
it by saying that there are no UFOs? Accordingly,
the Air Force wrote to Dean Edward U. Condon
of the University of Colorado advising him that he should debunk flying saucers once and for all. And Condon would do just that when
he summarized the full study years later, even though the individual
members of the study group strongly supported further investigation
of the UFO phenomenon.

> **HOW TO GET TO
> MCMINNVILLE BY AIR**
> All major airlines fly into
> Portland International
> Airport (PDX).

When the Condon Commission received the Trent photo negatives, their analysts set to work. But their expert skeptics couldn't find
a conventional explanation for the object in the photos. They looked
for ways the photos could be duplicated, but they found that unless
the Trents had constructed a very exact model and set up a plate shot
against which to photograph the model and brush in or out details
for light and shadow, this photo could not be debunked. Many of the
techniques available to amateur photo hoaxers in the 1960s weren't
available a decade earlier, especially to people who were not photo
professionals. So the Condon committee endorsed the photos as real.

ONGOING PROS AND CONS

Now fast-forward to 1975, twelve years after the negatives were sent to the Condon Committee investigators and a quarter of a century after Paul Trent had handed them over to Powell at the McMinnville newspaper. After the UPI had returned the negatives to the *McMinnville Register*, the editor kept them in his possession, not informing Paul Trent that they had been returned. In 1975, U.S. Navy physicist Dr. Bruce Maccabee—the same man who would gain fame as the analyst of the Gulf Breeze photos and again as the analyst for the Phoenix lights photos in the 1990s—discovered the negatives at the McMinnville newspaper and analyzed them.

Maccabee said that the negatives and their prints, on the basis of his analysis of light and shadow and proportion of subject to background, indicated that the photos were of a real object. He suggested that even trying to duplicate the photos would be difficult because of the way the light played off the subject and cast shadows.

Five years later, the late arch-debunker Phil Klass (who, as it turned out, not only wrote for *Aviation Week* but also worked for the CIA) came out with his own analysis of the photos. He argued that the odd light and shadows in the photos pinned them as obvious hoaxes. Klass said that the angle of sunlight was all wrong for an early evening photograph and said that if the Trents were lying about *when* the photo was taken, they were lying about the sighting. Klass said that the Trents had simply built a model of a flying saucer, suspended it on a nearly invisible wire from power lines nearby, and took the photograph. Unfortunately for the Trents, the angle of the sun and the shadow belied their story, so indicating to Klass that the photo and the story were hoaxed.

Not so, argued Maccabee again: the object in the photo was too far away from the power lines to have been suspended from them and the shadows, analyzed carefully, showed that they comported with the Trents' story.

Today, the photos still remain a mystery with skeptics debunking them as hoaxes and UFO researchers arguing that these photos are some of the most reliable examples of photo evidence of UFOs ever made public.

▶ UFO EVENTS

In May of every year there is a widely attended conference and parade in McMinnville celebrating the anniversary of the Trent photos. Along with serious discussions of the photos and their place in American UFO history, there is a costume parade and party with attendees dressing up as their favorite UFO/extraterrestrial and science fiction heroes. There are plenty of Darth Vaders and Yodas, lots of alien grays, and no small gathering of Klingons and Star Fleet personnel. Of all the UFO anniversary celebrations in the United States—with the sole exception of the July Roswell anniversary—none is more attended or celebrated than McMinnville.

▶ PLACES TO STAY

Red Lion Inn & Suites McMinnville
2535 NE Cumulus Avenue
McMinnville, Oregon

Best Western Vineyard Inn & Motel
2035 S Highway 99W
McMinnville, Oregon

Hotel Oregon
310 NE Evans Street
McMinnville, Oregon

Motel 6 McMinnville
2065 SW Highway 99W
McMinnville, Oregon

Comfort Inn & Suites
2520 SE Stratus Avenue
McMinnville, Oregon

Safari Motor Inn McMinnville
381 NE Highway Hwy 99W
McMinnville, Oregon

▶ RESTAURANTS

Bistro Maison
729 NE Third Street
McMinnville, Oregon

Thistle
228 North Evans Street
McMinnville, Oregon

La Rambla
238 NE Third Street
McMinnville, Oregon

Thai Country Restaurant
707 NE Third Street
McMinnville, Oregon

Nick's Italian Café
521 NE Third Street
McMinnville, Oregon

■ McMinnville, Oregon

CHAPTER TWENTY
THE GREAT LAKES UFOs

Sometimes UFO incidents are more than just sightings or reports of landings. Sometimes, what credible or professional witnesses see in the sky is corroborated by what radar operators also see and track on their screens. When that happens, science tells us to presume that the objects being witnessed are real and not just witness confusion or radar anomalies—especially when the movements witnesses see are the same movements observed on radar. This was the case over Holland, Michigan, and five other locations on March 8, 1994, as local 911 dispatchers tracked UFOs across Michigan, Ohio, and into Illinois.

LIGHTS ABOVE THE LAKE

The long and, for 911 first responders, horrendous night began when a police officer saw multiple lights over an area neighboring Holland, Michigan. At the same time in the evening, residents from other areas adjacent to Holland also reported strange red, blue, and green lights in the sky. Soon, calls from witnesses reporting lights began deluging the local 911 dispatchers with their observations. By 9:15 that night, dispatchers were thoroughly aware that *something* was in the air on the eastern shore of Lake Michigan. The call activity became so intense that for a time, local dispatchers reported that their boards were jammed and couldn't take any more calls. By 9:45, hundreds of

witnesses had called 911. Police units on patrol and at the very locations where witnesses reported the strings of lights in the skies were
also reporting that they were witnessing lights crossing the sky.

The Holland, Michigan area is right across the lake from Chicago's O'Hare Airport, one of the busiest in the nation. Chicago Center
controls the flights coming into the area and the residents in western
Michigan are no strangers to jets making their
approach into Chicago. They are used to seeing the lights from conventional aircraft as well
as from helicopters in the sky. But the lights
they were observing that night, according to
one of the witnesses in Holland, were nothing
like aircraft lights. First of all, this witness said,
these lights were all the wrong colors. Rather
than the bright navigation lights on commer-
cial jets and helicopters, these were strings of lights almost like Christ-
mas tree lights. They were all colors: red, green, and blue. Moreover,
the lights didn't just remain fixed, they seemed to be coming together,
arranging themselves in geometric patterns, and then splitting apart.

HOW TO GET TO HOLLAND, MICHIGAN BY AIR
All major airlines service Detroit Metropolitan Wayne County Airport (DTW). You can also fly into Chicago's O'Hare International Airport (ORD) or Midway International Airport (MDW).

Government agencies even confirmed that the lights couldn't be
planes. Due to the alarming number of calls, a 911 dispatch operator
wanted to see if there were any planes in the air that night. Calls to the
FAA brought back the answer that nothing that might be in the air
that night could account for the strings of lights that witnesses were
reporting. Frustrated, the dispatcher called radar operators at the
National Weather Service. These operators were constantly at their
consoles, and if anything anomalous were turning up on their screens,
they should be able to report it.

Meanwhile, police units followed the lights traveling at an altitude
of about 1,000 to 5,000 feet. The more the calls came in from wit-

nesses, the more police units were dispatched to the witness locations and were able to spot the lights in the sky. By 9:45 P.M., units from across towns in southwestern Michigan were following the lights in the sky like a scene out of a Steven Spielberg movie.

BELIEVE YOUR EYES; BELIEVE THE RADAR

When the 911 operator spoke to operator Jack Bushong at the National Weather Service, he was able to confirm that what witnesses were observing from the ground were now targets on his radar scope. Finally by 10 P.M., Holland Township police officer Jeff Vellhouse was patched directly in to Muskegon, Michigan, National Weather Service radar operator Bushong by the 911 dispatch officer. Their conversation, recorded on 911 tapes, is perhaps one of the most important

VISITING HOLLAND

Holland, Michigan is dotted with camping facilities, streams, and ponds. There are many activities for families who visit the area to see where the UFOs were spotted, where they flew, and the routes they took. As its name suggests, Holland is a Dutch-themed area with a unique shopping center, tulip festival, and one of the most interesting high-tech adventure parks in the Midwest.

The Lost City in the Holland Town Center
12330 James Street
Holland, Michigan

Nelis' Dutch Village
12350 James Street
Holland, Michigan

Veldheer's Tulip Farm
12755 Quincy Street
Holland, Michigan

The Holland Museum
31 West 10th Street
Holland, Michigan

The Holland Aquatic Center
550 Maple Avenue
Holland, Michigan

Tulip Time Festival
238 South River Avenue
Holland, Michigan

pieces of evidence in modern American UFO history: it documents that officer Vellhouse was observing in person an object performing the same maneuvers that Bushong was observing on his radar screen. Their conversation has become lore in UFO research. In fact, a former director for the Center for UFO Studies, Professor Michael Swords, has confirmed that he personally interviewed Bushong and that the relationship between the objects Bushong tracked on his radar and the objects that Vellhouse tracked from the ground are probably the most important pieces of evidence for the existence of unidentified aerial phenomena.

As Vellhouse reported the objects changing position, Bushong became more and more intense as he confirmed those changes on his radarscope. At first, Bushong said the objects were disappearing and then reappearing on the radar. Then he said that when he went to a closer range, he could make the objects out clearly and they were moving in ways no conventional aircraft could move. He clocked them moving at over a thousand to 1,500 miles an hour, an unheard of speed for anything other than supersonic military aircraft. Vellhouse said that the objects were coming together and then splitting apart, and

COMPARING NOTES

Vellhouse: "[Bushong] said he had three things on his radar, and they were in a triangular shape. He said they hovered over Holland and moved southwest. He said that one would move out of the triangular pattern, then move back in."

Bushong: "There were three and sometimes four blips, and they weren't planes. Planes show as pinpoints on the scope, these were the size of half a thumbnail. They were from 5 to 12,000 feet at times, moving all over the place. Three were moving toward Chicago. I never saw anything like it before, not even when I'm doing severe weather."

■ Holland, Michigan

Bushong asked, "what is this?" Looking at his scope, he blurted out with panic in his voice, "Oh my God. What is this?" He had never seen anything like this before.

When Vellhouse said that he saw an actual formation of lights, Bushong responded that he saw "three" that had formed themselves into a triangle. As Vellhouse described the lights turning from red to green, Bushong was at a loss to explain the kind of energy the radar returns were showing him. They were very strong, he said, intense, but not at all like an aircraft. And they were heading west toward the Chicago Center control towers for approaches to O'Hare Airport. For the next few minutes, 911, Vellhouse, and Bushong tracked the objects in the sky and the blips on his radar as they crossed the shore of western Michigan and moved out over the lake. And then the sky was empty.

DENYING THE OBVIOUS

Even though Bushong made tapes of the event, they were destroyed by the National Weather Service. The FAA also denies there having been any targets in the air that night that the National Weather Service could have picked up. Yet the 911 dispatch tapes survived and were played on the radio; they are now available on the Internet at: *www .ufocasebook.com/hollandmichigantranscript.html* for folks to read for themselves.

In subsequent interviews, Bushong confirmed what he saw on his radar that night, however, the manager of the National Weather Service for the Michigan area completely denied any relationship between the objects that Bushong saw on his scope that night and the objects that Vellhouse reported to his 911 dispatcher. It was only with the release of the transcript of the dispatch recording and Bushong's interviews with Professor Swords of CUFOS and his appearance on a 2008 documentary that confirmed the events of that night, Bushong's recording of them, and Bushong's actual sketches of the positions of the blips on his scope, their size, and their direction.

It took fourteen years for the solid evidence to substantiate what residents in Holland, Michigan saw, what police tracked in their vehicles, and what the National Weather Service radar confirmed. Despite the denials by the military, by the FAA, and by the National Weather Service, solid and professional research by CUFOS, Dr. Michael Swords, and by UFO investigators in Michigan finally cataloged and presented the evidence of one of the most intriguing and multiple-witnessed UFO sightings since the 1952 UFO invasion of Washington, DC.

▶ PLACES TO STAY

Haworth Inn and Conference Center
225 College Avenue
Holland, Michigan

City Flats Hotel
61 East 7th Street
Holland, Michigan

Hampton Inn Holland
12427 Felch Street
Holland, Michigan

Fairfield Inn Holland
2854 West Shore Drive
Holland, Michigan

Doubletree Hotel Holland
650 East 24th Street
Holland, Michigan

Holiday Inn Express
12381 Felch Street
Holland, Michigan

Days Inn Holland
717 Hastings Avenue, U.S. 31 &
32nd Street
Holland, Michigan

▶ RESTAURANTS

Alpenrose
4 East 8th Street
Holland, Michigan

Butch's
44 East 8th Street
Holland, Michigan

New Holland Brewing Company
66 East 8th Street
Holland, Michigan

Boatwerks
216 Van Raalte Avenue
Holland, Michigan

Pereddies
447 Washington Square
Holland, Michigan

84 East
84 East 8th Street
Holland, Michigan

Via Maria Trattoria
13 West 7th Street
Holland, Michigan

INDEX

ABOUT THE AUTHOR

Lead host and consulting producer of History Channel's *UFO Hunters*, radio personality, and *New York Times* bestselling author **William J. Birnes** is currently a guest expert on History Channel's *Ancient Aliens*. Birnes cohosts the weekly radio show *Future Theater* on the Clark Radio Network and Talk Stream Live with his wife— *UFO Magazine* and Filament Books editor-in-chief Nancy Hayfield. He has written and edited over twenty-five books and encyclopedias in the fields of human behavior, true crime, current affairs, history, psychology, business, computing, and the paranormal. His books include *Space Wars* and *Counter Space, Haunting of America, Haunting of Twentieth-Century America*, and *Journey to the Light*.

Birnes is the editorial director of his own literary series with *Coast to Coast AM* host George Noory. He is president of the book production company Shadow Lawn Press, publisher and president of Filament Electronic Books, and the publisher of *UFO Magazine*. Three of his coauthored books have been turned into cable features: *The Day After Roswell, The Riverman*, and *The Haunting of the President*. His title *Black Dahlia Avenger*, also a bestseller, is currently in development at New Line.

Birnes has appeared on *Good Morning America*; *Dateline, NBC*; *Entertainment Tonight*; *Coast to Coast AM*; *UFOs in Russia*; *USOs: Underwater Submersible Objects*; and *Black Box UFOs*. He had a featured role in the film *Occam's Razor* in 1999, and was featured in a Canadian Broadcasting Company documentary on the O.J. Simpson murder trial in 1995. Birnes's first cable feature as producer was *When Husbands Cheat*, for Lifetime Television with Hearst Entertainment Television.

A National Endowment for the Humanities Post Doctoral Fellow, grants judge for the National Endowment for the Arts, and a law school graduate, Birnes received his PhD from New York University in 1974 while he was an assistant professor of English on the graduate faculty at Trenton State College. He completed his post-doctoral work under a Lily Foundation Fellowship at the University of Pennsylvania. He started Shadow Lawn Press in 1983; the company introduced the television retrospective cookbooks *The Gilligan's Island Cookbook*, *The Brady Bunch Cookbook*, *The Bewitched Cookbook*, and *The Star Trek Cookbook* as well as the how-to titles *Cheaper and Better* and *Zapcraft*.

Birnes and his wife live in New Jersey and Los Angeles.

PHOTO CREDITS

Page 2 courtesy of Kathleen Mardin

Page 7 courtesy of Kathleen Mardin

Page 11 courtesy of Dr. Bruce Cornet

Page 24 reprinted from *UFO Magazine*

Page 34 courtesy of *UFO Magazine*

Page 45 courtesy of Stan Gordon

Page 58 courtesy of Connie Menger

Page 61 courtesy *UFO Magazine*

Page 63 courtesy of *UFO Magazine*

Page 71 courtesy of *UFO Magazine*

Page 87 courtesy of Frank Feschino, Jr., all rights reserved

Page 96 courtesy of Dr. Bruce Maccabee

Page 99 courtesy of Dr. Bruce Maccabee

Page 103 courtesy of Dr. Bruce Maccabee

Page 109 courtesy of *UFO Magazine*

Page 123 by Steve Nigg; courtesy of Bill Birnes

Page 124 courtesy of *UFO Magazine*

Page 129 courtesy of *UFO Magazine*

Page 132 courtesy of *UFO Magazine*

Page 141 courtesy of *UFO Magazine*

Page 151 courtesy of Tom Carey and Donald Schmitt, *Witness to Roswell*

Page 157 courtesy of Tom Carey and Donald Schmitt, *Witness to Roswell* and *UFO Magazine*

Page 159 courtesy of Tom Carey and Donald Schmitt, *Witness to Roswell*

Page 161 courtesy of Tom Carey and Donald Schmitt, *Witness to Roswell*

Page 169 courtesy of the Magruder family and *UFO Magazine*

Page 170 courtesy of *UFO Magazine*

Page 176 courtesy of *UFO Magazine* files

Page 205 by Paul Trent, courtesy of Dr. Bruce Maccabee

BEYOND HERE

Sure, this world is fascinating, but *what's beyond is even more alluring...*

Want a place to share stories and experiences about all things strange and unusual? From UFOs and apparitions to dream interpretation, the Tarot, astrology, and more, the **BEYOND HERE** blog is the newest hot spot for paranormal activity!

Visit the BEYOND HERE blog today at
www.adamsmedia.com/blog/paranormal